Can I Believe?

Christianity for the Hesitant

JOHN G. STACKHOUSE, JR.

OXFORD
UNIVERSITY PRESS

OXFORD
UNIVERSITY PRESS

Oxford University Press is a department of the University of Oxford. It furthers the University's objective of excellence in research, scholarship, and education by publishing worldwide. Oxford is a registered trade mark of Oxford University Press in the UK and certain other countries.

Published in the United States of America by Oxford University Press
198 Madison Avenue, New York, NY 10016, United States of America.

Library of Congress Cataloging-in-Publication Data
Names: Stackhouse, John G. (John Gordon), 1960– author.
Title: Can I believe? : Christianity for the hesitant / John G. Stackhouse, Jr.
Description: New York, NY, United States of America :
Oxford University Press, 2020. |
Includes bibliographical references and index.
Identifiers: LCCN 2020016982 (print) | LCCN 2020016983 (ebook) |
ISBN 9780190922856 (paperback) | ISBN 9780190922870 (epub)
Subjects: LCSH: Apologetics. | Christianity—Essence, genius, nature.
Classification: LCC BT1103 .S726 2020 (print) |
LCC BT1103 (ebook) | DDC 239—dc23
LC record available at https://lccn.loc.gov/2020016982
LC ebook record available at https://lccn.loc.gov/2020016983

1 3 5 7 9 8 6 4 2

Printed by Sheridan Books, Inc., United States of America

Praise for *Can I Believe?*

Here is a book for everyone who wants their life to be in harmony with reality. If you are ready for your beliefs—and your reasons for choosing them—to be challenged to the core, then you should read this.

—Andrew Briggs, Professor of
Nanomaterials, University of Oxford

John Stackhouse strikes a brilliant balance. As a devoted Christian, he has the confidence to proselytize, yet he also has the humility to respect my intelligence, dignity, and humanity as a non-Christian. Be not afraid of his invitation. In our age of raging dogmas, who asks for simple consideration without expectation of outcome? Stackhouse, that's who. In more ways than one, this book is a counter-cultural delight.

— Irshad Manji, Founder,
Moral Courage Project

Intelligent, erudite, and witty, this book is a guide to answering with integrity the most important question of our lives: "What kind of life is worthy of our humanity?" That's the kind of "believing" Stackhouse explores: the knowledge and trust needed for embarking upon a comprehensive way of life.

— Miroslav Volf, Henry B. Wright Professor
of Theology and Director of the Yale Center
for Faith and Culture, Yale University

for Cynthia

Let us suppose we possess parts of a novel or a symphony. Someone now brings us a newly discovered piece of manuscript and says, "This is the missing part of the work. This is the chapter on which the whole plot of the novel really turned. This is the main theme of the symphony." Our business would be to see whether the new passage, if admitted to the central place which the discoverer claimed for it, did actually illuminate all the parts we had already seen and "pull them together."

. . . If it were genuine then at every fresh hearing of the music or every fresh reading of the book, we should find it settling down, making itself more at home and eliciting significance from all sorts of details in the whole work which we had hitherto neglected. Even though the new central chapter or main theme contains great difficulties in itself, we should still think it genuine provided that it continually removed difficulties elsewhere.

—C. S. Lewis

In what other field of study would so many people reach so dismissive conclusions on the basis of so little knowledge as outsiders are comfortable with in disregarding Christian truth?

—Margaret Avison

Contents

Acknowledgments   ix

Introduction   1

1 How to Decide   5
   Deciding about Religion   5
   What Is a Religion?   7
   Arriving at Options   10
   Investigating Religions   13
   Can We Actually Know?   15
   Knowledge as a Condition for Faith—and Vice Versa   17
   Religious Faith   21
   How to Decide about Religion   24

2 What Is Christianity?   33
   Introduction: A Fourfold Scheme   33
   The Strangeness of Christianity   35
   What Is Real: Creation   40
   What Is Best: Shalom   44
   What Is Wrong: Sin and Evil   51
   What Can Be Done: Initial Options   61
   What Can Be Done: Religious Options   67
   What Can Be Done: The Christian View   72
   What Can Be Done: Our Side   83

3 Why Does Anyone Believe?   91
   Since Christianity Focuses on Christ   91
   Historical Grounds   95
   Philosophical Grounds   114
   Ethical and Pragmatic Grounds   128
   Aesthetic Grounds   140
   Psychological and Experiential Grounds   146

4 Why Not Believe?   157
   The Problem of Particularity   157
   The Problem of Evil   166

5 What Now?   175

Notes   181

Acknowledgments

I have been inspired and informed by many exemplars of such conversation about Christianity, especially classic thinkers Blaise Pascal, G. K. Chesterton, Dorothy Sayers, and C. S. Lewis, and contemporaries Os Guinness, Al Plantinga, Steve Evans, Rodney Stark, and Tom Wright. Mentors Mark Noll, Martin Marty, Nick Wolterstorff, and the late David Martin have shown me that very, very smart people could be faithful, even fervent, Christians—doubts and all.

Crandall University's enlightened approach to research leaves gave me the time to write the first draft of this book. I appreciatively recall the fruitful conversations I have enjoyed on these questions with students and faculty members at Crandall as well as at Canadian Mennonite University, Carey Baptist College (Auckland), Christ College (Sydney), Fudan University, Harding University, Harvard University, Lakehead University, Morling College, Pepperdine University, Queen's University (Kingston), Regent College, the Scots College (Sydney), Seoul Theological University, Stanford University, Tabor College (Adelaide), Torch Trinity Graduate School, Tyndale Theological Seminary (Toronto), the University of British Columbia, the University of Lethbridge, the University of Manitoba, the University of Northern British Columbia, the University of Otago, the University of Virginia, the University of Windsor, Wheaton College, Wuhan University, and Zhejiang University.

Friends Steve Baughman, Irshad Manji, Mickey Maudlin, Jonathan Merritt, and Randall Rauser kindly gave me advice at different stages of the writing of this book, and the faults that remain are due to their advice not being good enough. (I appreciate their trying, nonetheless.) Fair spouse, my beloved wife of four decades, has had almost nothing to do with my writing, but she has done her best with me. I, and my books, are much the better for that tireless effort.

Finally, this is the sixth volume I have published under the gentle, if also exacting, hand of editor Cynthia Read. Cynthia has been an adviser of preternatural wisdom who has become a treasured friend. It is my honor, therefore, to dedicate this book to her.

Feast of St. Michael and All Angels 2019

Can I Believe?

Introduction

Take your pick: it's a target-rich environment.

Creation of the entire universe in a week. A talking serpent and a death-dealing fruit. A worldwide flood. A fugitive nation hurrying on dry ground across the floor of the Red Sea. A city's walls falling flat at the sound of trumpets. The sun standing still. Any one of a hundred implausibilities that would make a reasonable person say, "Come on. Get serious."

The miracles come fast and furious in Jesus's career: from walking on water to feeding a crowd from a single lunch to casting out demons to raising the dead. And then he himself gets raised from the dead—and is worshipped as God, by people who knew him first as—a carpenter. Really?

Maybe it's the ethics that, for all their familiarity, seem absurd. Turn the other cheek. Don't even look at a woman with desire. Blessed are the meek. Love your enemies. One doesn't have to be Nietzsche to wonder if something truly weird is being taught.

Maybe it's the *lack* of ethics. Exhibit A: the Crusades. Exhibit B: the Inquisition. And then there's imperialism and colonialism and the white man's burden and Manifest Destiny. And sexism. And racism. And child abuse. And homophobia.

Too much involvement in politics. Too little. Opposition to science. *Legitimation* of science—and the consequent despoliation of the earth through rapacious technology. The indictment goes on and on, with reason after reason to be disaffected with, even repelled by, Christianity.

How could any sensible, decent person believe it? This book focuses on this single question. But let's make it harder. How, in fact, have *two billion* people found this very strange story, and this deeply checkered heritage, compelling?

Some of those two billion aren't very bright, to be sure. Many of them have evident psychological problems. Not a few seem to be in it for the money and power that any popular movement can offer.

But all two billion of them? Across all lines of culture and class, ethnicity and language, time and place? Ivy League professors and Oxbridge dons? Nobel and Pulitzer Prize winners? CERN and NIH directors? How can *those* people believe?

That's the question. And if it's your question, this book is for you.

We'll begin by introducing the fundamental matters any reasonable person should consider in trying to make her way through the bewildering marketplace of competing philosophies and religions. How could someone possibly make a rational, responsible choice amid the welter of the world's alternatives?

Then the conversation turns to Christianity, at once the most popular and yet perhaps the most unlikely explanation of reality of any of the major ideological options that have appeared in world history. We'll try to get this story straight, amid all the distorted versions of Christianity that have emerged over two millennia. We'll find that Christians don't need to believe some of the outlandish things they have been taught they should believe. We'll also find that the Christian story possesses a certain logic: it isn't just one bizarre wonder after another.

We'll conclude, however, that Christian faith remains very strange. That poor man groaning on a Roman cross is supposed to be the Savior of the World. Preposterous, isn't it? Only extraordinarily strong grounds could make such a claim believable. So we will survey a brief catalog of the grounds those two billion Christians have found convincing: from history to philosophy, from aesthetics to ethics, from hardheaded rationality to, yes, mystical experience.

Ah, but what about the counterarguments? Lots of people, after all, have encountered Christianity, been raised in it or otherwise convinced by it, and yet eventually have found it incredible, even revolting. We'll take an honest look at those, too—some of them along the way, and the Two Biggest Ones at the end. How could we not?

And then—what? You'll be entirely convinced and convert on the spot?

Not likely.

You will, however, perhaps understand more clearly what Christianity does and doesn't claim, and what Christianity does and doesn't offer. You will be in a better position to decide whether you can, in fact, believe. And if that seems worth your while, then I trust you'll read on.

1

How to Decide

Deciding about Religion

"And that's how I became a Christian."

Two billion Christians in the world, and every one of them tells a similar story: "One day I decided to choose a religion. So I put out the dog, made myself a pot of tea, sat down to read all the pertinent material, had a good think, and made an informed choice."

One can be confident that precisely no one has come to Christian faith that way, or ever will. Selecting among the vast array of religious and philosophical options available today isn't like solving a crossword puzzle, buying a new appliance, or selecting the right insurance policy.

But what *is* it like? How is it possible to come to a reasonable and confident decision about it all?

For lots of people, "reasonable" is the last thing religion is. Physics is about reason: about facts and evidence and logical argument. Sociology is about reason. Politics *should* be about reason. Religion, however, is about mere belief, about faith, about gut feelings and poorly described experiences and overactive consciences.

Why *do* religious people believe the things they do? Why do religious people commit themselves to a particular way of life different from that of their neighbors? Why do religious people trust their holy books and holy clergy to tell them truths they cannot otherwise discover?

Maybe religious people are just credulous. Maybe they just grow up in a particular religion and never question it. Maybe they are psychologically needy and gravitate toward domineering personalities and simplistic rulebooks. Maybe they are cowards who shrink from facing reality and withdraw into comforting illusions fostered by similarly deluded weaklings or, worse, exploitative charlatans.

But *all* of them? All four, five, six billion religious people around the world—and many more throughout the ages? War-toughened soldiers, sober-minded scientists, hardheaded executives, seen-it-all nurses, sensitive artists, erudite scholars, and courageous explorers—are the religious among them (and there are many) to be dismissed so easily?

Many thoughtful people's minds house a conceptual jungle about religion. The jungle is particularly thick around how people form, or should form, religious convictions. Words such as "faith" and "belief" and "truth" and "knowledge" and "reason" and "evidence" and "argument" and "testimony" and "experience" all blur together into a fog that makes religion mysterious, and perhaps off-putting. And when science seems instead to be all about brightly lit laboratories and clearly marked instruments and precisely taken measurements and rigorously tested findings, no wonder so many people set religion over against science and judge religion badly deficient by comparison. Sociologist Charles Selengut speaks for many:

> Religious faith is different than other commitments and the rules and directives of religion are understood by the faithful to be entirely outside ordinary social rules and interactions. . . . For the faithful, religious judgments are self-legitimating; they are true and proper rules not because they can be proven to be so by philosophers or because they have social benefits but because they emanate from a divine source. Ordinary judgment, canons of logic, and evaluation of behavior simply do not apply to religious activity. . . . Faith and religious behavior are not based upon science, practical politics, or Western notions of logic or efficiency but on following the word of God regardless of the

cost. Holy wars . . . may not be amenable to logical and rational solutions. Faithful holy warriors, whether in Afghanistan, Israel, Palestine, or Florida, live in a psychic and social reality different from the world inhabited by secularized people.[1]

However, if this were so, then no scientist would be a religious believer—unless suffering from some sadly compromised mental and emotional state. Yet lots of apparently functional scientists are Christians, Jews, Muslims, or faithful members of another religion. So what is religious belief, and how can a serious person hold it?

In what follows, I'm going to try to demonstrate what will initially seem an odd, and oddly mild, claim—namely, that religious belief is best understood as belief about religious subjects. Nothing about religious belief is utterly different from the way we make up our minds about other matters. It is a way of thinking that is appropriate to its subject matter and is paralleled in obvious ways by similar beliefs about similar things. Christian faith in particular, I intend to show, is not the result of some bizarre thought process completely different from how we decide about scientific or historical or ethical matters. It is the outcome of what we might call generic rationality. And inasmuch as faith has a personal element—belief *in* God, not just forming correct beliefs *about* God—Christian faith is like our trusting other persons, not some supra-rational miracle completely different from the rest of our experience.

Let's begin, then, by defining what we mean by *religion*. Then we'll set out what it means to think about religion in a responsible way.

What Is a Religion?

A thing or an idea should be evaluated according to its kind and its fitness for purpose. A horse can be assessed in terms of its strength for pulling, or its speed for running, or its agility for roping, among other qualities. An automobile can be prized as a practical conveyance, as a racing machine, or as a status symbol. Minivans, roadsters, and limousines each have their place. A person can earn regard variously for her wisdom, her beauty, her generosity, her endurance, her enthusiasm, and so on, depending on the context. How, then, does one begin to consider a religion? What is it, and what is it for?

When the word "religion" is used, most people likely will think of God, gods, or at least some sense of the supernatural. There is the ordinary world of our daily experience, and then there is whatever is "up there" or "beyond" or "the other": whatever is *additional*, and perhaps transcendent. Scholars of religion, however, tend to find this definition too narrow. For one thing, most of us expect to find Buddhism, Daoism, and Confucianism on a list of religions, and indeed they show up regularly in textbook surveys of world religions. Yet important forms of each of these traditions either deny the existence of deities and a supernatural realm or are largely indifferent to them. For another thing, religions typically affect much or all of everyday life, not just some sort of special "religious" life practiced on special holy days in special holy places.

The *functional* definition of religion considers what religions typically *do*. A religion, in this view, is what orients, motivates, and structures the central zone of life—for an individual or a group. Our *functional* religion stems from our fundamental beliefs and values. Our religion is whatever constitutes the ultimate concern (to borrow a term from Paul Tillich) of an individual or a group, whatever is the core of life around which everything else is wound.

A religion therefore consists of a particular set of beliefs (what to think), values (what to esteem or despise), and practices (what to do or avoid). Articulated sets of beliefs, values, and practices constitute what might be called "proper noun" religions: Judaism, Shinto, Buddhism, and the like. Islam, for example, teaches certain things to be true ("There is no god but God, and Muhammad is his prophet"), encourages the cultivation of specific concerns and emotions (especially submission to God: the word "muslim" means "submitted one"), and (thus) prescribes certain actions (such as the Five Pillars of Islam, which include recitation of the creed, daily prayers, pilgrimage to Mecca, and so on).

Clearly Christianity, Hinduism, and Daoism function in this way. But so do Marxism, secular humanism, and pragmatism. So do hedonism, status seeking, and other forms of egotism. To be sure, some objects of devotion are idiosyncratic: "He looks after that car religiously," we might say. I remember a startling television program that profiled a middle-aged man living in Oklahoma whose functional religion was (although neither he nor the interviewer put it this way) supporting the University of Oklahoma Sooners football team. This man wore only clothes patterned in Sooners red and white. His house was red and white brick on the outside, and red and white throughout the interior—accented only by pigskin brown. The white handset of his phone rested in a plastic football. His walls were covered with Sooners posters. His work schedule was arranged around the Sooners' schedule—from spring camp to bowl games. And, for a while, he sported letters spelling out S-O-O-N-E-R-S in red across his front teeth, until his wife made his dentist whiten them again. This man reminds us that "fan" is an abbreviation for "fanatic."[2]

One might choose to live within the structures of an "organized" religion such as Christianity. Or one might prefer to live according to what sociologists sometimes call "DIY religion," "religion à la carte," or "informal religion"—the contemporary mode of picking elements from the smorgasbord of religions and putting together a package of beliefs, values, and practices for oneself. *Whatever* it is, however, that gives meaning, purpose, direction, and intensity to life; whatever gets us going in the morning; whatever drives us forward; whatever consoles us in misery; whatever stands at the center of our lives and gives us our definition of success—functionally speaking, that is our religion.

So how do we responsibly come up with such a religion?

Arriving at Options

There are three possible routes to a religion. The first might be to gather all the pertinent information, muse upon it, and see what emerges, what occurs to you as the best explanation of—everything. That's what do-it-yourselfers do—or, at least, that's what they think they do.

It is rather a large task, however: to investigate everything pertinent to the well-lived life, weigh up all plausible interpretative options, and formulate a lasting, fruitful way of being in the world. And despite the apparently universal sense of competence in this field—everyone seems to feel entirely comfortable opining about religion, no matter what education and experience they have or haven't had—the thoughtful person will pause to wonder just how she is to get her conceptual arms around, well, everything.

It turns out that the construct-your-own-religion syndrome shows up only in a particular cultural place: modern affluent countries deeply shaped by the Christian religion.[3] All the choices we think we are freely and sovereignly making about religion are in fact taking place in a complex cultural ecosystem in which the questions to answer and the problems to solve are relatively few, compared to the vast majority of human beings, who have had to confront life on earth with much less to go on. To start truly from scratch puts us back with the Aegean philosophers of the pre-Socratic era, or those of ancient India or China, and who wants to do two or three millennia's worth of thinking if it's not absolutely necessary? Why not consider whether other people have come up with plausible answers already and see what we think of those?

The second option therefore is to explore all the religions of the world, evaluate them, and decide which is the best. When making this assessment, we do well to consider each option according to what a religion is supposed to do. Fundamentally, I suggest, a religion does three things: it tells us the way things are, it tells us how to respond best to the way things are, and it gives us a community of like-minded people to encourage and instruct us. We can borrow from the academic study of religion a nice phrase for these three elements: "a creed, a code, and a community."

How well, then, does any given religion serve as the center of (a) human life? How well does it explain the world and our place in it? How well does it recognize our highest good? How well does it diagnose what keeps us from that good? How well does it prescribe the solution to our problems? And how much help does it give us in reaching that highest good?

If we attempt to compare and evaluate all the extant religious options, we encounter several difficulties. Religions are generally deeply complex things, with complicated inner workings, bewildering varieties within each species, and customs of speech and conduct that can take years to understand, let alone to master. I know experts who have taken a lifetime to thoroughly understand a single religion, and I know a few who have thoroughly understood two and even three. I know no one who claims to be an expert in more than three. Most religions are just that difficult to fully comprehend.

Even if you could gather an appropriate amount and kind of data on two or more religions, how would you decide which data are in fact appropriate? On what basis would you confidently collect one sort of data (say, about basic doctrines) and set aside as relatively unimportant other data (such as the way believers dress for worship)? Isn't there an implicit value judgment involved here ("belief is more important than costume") that is simply presupposed according to the bias of the inquirer? It does not "naturally" emerge from the study itself. Or perhaps it does, in the sense that perhaps neither religion A nor religion B seems to take clothing as seriously as it takes ideas. Yet even then, another inquirer might come along who is deeply interested in how a religion views and treats the body, and thus see this lack of interest in clothing as in fact significant. Perhaps such an inquirer might then judge both religion A and religion B to be hopelessly deficient and move on to the options that do pay attention to clothing. How can we know with confidence what really matters?

The data to be explained—namely, all of reality, which might include supernatural beings and even a God whose nature, thoughts, and actions transcend our understanding—appear to be extremely numerous and in some cases profoundly complex. The "mapping reality" part of comparing and assessing religions is impossible to undertake with hope of anything approaching a confident conclusion.

More problems arise as we attend to the ethical dimension of such a project. What universal standard of ultimate goodness, of the summum bonum, can one use to evaluate religious options? It is relatively easy to decide what an automobile is for in any given instance, and to then make a decision as to which candidate fulfills that purpose best—although experts might disagree. It is less easy, but possible, to decide what a human being is for in a particular instance and appraise candidates accordingly: Who jumps the highest? Who plays the violin best? Who writes the tightest computer code? In the case of religion, however, what definition of religion's ultimate purpose sets the standard? Is the primary objective of religion to eradicate suffering? To achieve individual bliss? To provide social order? Perhaps it is to keep the workers docile and compliant, or to introduce select individuals to ultimate truth. Is it to rescue spirits from their material prisons? Is it to form a people for fellowship with a Supreme Being, leaving the rest for destruction?

This second approach, therefore, bristles with difficulties. The third approach is the one for which most people opt. List one's "live options" (as William James puts it) and proceed as follows: begin with studying the most promising option so that one sees it clearly; assess the best grounds for believing it; assess the best grounds for *not* believing it; and then adopt it, if it measures up, or move on, if it doesn't. That is what we'll do in the rest of this book in regard to the most popular option in world history, Christianity.

Before we begin, however, it would be well to consider a few more factors affecting our attempt to find the right religion.

Investigating Religions

How would someone properly explore a religion, not just as a matter of intellectual curiosity, but as a genuine possibility for guiding his or her life? Students in my courses on world religions sometimes come to me privately and ask just this question. "I'm interested in Baha'i," they might say. "How would I go beyond the introduction given in this course?"

I recommend they consult at least these three sets of resources. First, they should read a good introduction to the religion written by a reputable scholar who is trying neither to praise nor condemn. No such observer is completely unbiased, of course, but the good ones strive to be as accurate and even-handed as possible. Publishers of textbooks try to find such authors because the less controversial and more objective they are, the more *other* professors are likely to assign their books.

Second, inquirers should read the chief writings of the religion in question and one or more recommendations by leading apologists— to hear the religion in its own voices. Clergy and professors who teach this religion are probably the best guides to such literature.

Third, one should encounter the religion in its most loyal and impressive devotees. It's easy to make a mistake here: one might visit, for example, one of the many declining or moribund Christian churches in North America or Europe and come to false conclusions about the religion as a whole. "Well, if *that's* Christianity, so long!" Instead, try to find the most faithful and vibrant church, or mosque, or temple, or synagogue—one that is vitally living out the mainstream of that religion—and get to know believers who can help the inquirer understand the attractiveness of this religion. The objective is to encounter the religion at its best.

The attitude with which we approach this investigation is crucial. We must be both open and critical. If we are not sufficiently empathetic and not sufficiently vulnerable to changing our mind, if we are not truly willing to entertain the idea that these people might just be right—then we will not enter into that religion far enough to understand its essence. Our resistance acts as a kind of unhelpful buoyancy in our investigation, keeping us paddling on the surface when we should be diving deep. If we are not sufficiently critical, however, we will miss the religion's incongruities, contradictions, and perhaps even pathologies. We want to dive deep, yes, but not into unseen peril. And we need to be able to surface at any time. Some forms of religion are toxic, and while exploring, we need to keep our wits about us. Scholars of religion try to cultivate an attitude of "analytical empathy," a nicely poised tension of appreciation and critique. So should every other serious investigator.

The prudent inquirer also will be clear as to the realistic goal of such investigation. She shouldn't be looking for the One Perfect Religion. That would be like looking for the One Perfect Job, or the One Perfect Spouse, or the One Perfect Political Party. Whenever human beings are involved, things are imperfect. She would also avoid fixating on a particular attractive element in a religion, but rather step back to take things in as a whole. A religion is to be evaluated and embraced as an *entire way of life*, not just as a spur to political action, or as a soothing therapy, or as a safe social group for the kids.

Instead, she should be looking for the *best option overall*. Furthermore, she should recognize that whatever conclusion she comes to will be a "hypothesis," her best judgment on the matter to date. She may embrace that conclusion with fervor, but she ought to maintain a genuine and lively critical openness in the future just in case a better option comes along.

This may sound like vulgar consumerism, an attitude grossly out of place in the realm of the sacred. It may seem that I am advocating withholding a full commitment on matters to which we ought to be fully committed indeed. But commitment that closes itself off from any possibility of correction or improvement is not faith, but fanaticism. Wisdom recognizes the limitations in all of our thinking, including our thinking about religion, and leaves the door open, always, just in case a saving word needs to reach us.

So are we now adrift in a sea of possibilities, leaving us only with our shifting impressions of the world? How can one lead a life of firm commitment like *that*?

Can We Actually Know?

Each of us must decide for ourselves. We have to do so according to whatever wisdom we have learned and whatever happen to be the inclinations of our hearts. What else can we do? As a Christian, I believe that God makes clear to people in some elementary but unmistakable way what really matters in life, and people choose either to honor that wisdom and follow God's way or to walk instead their own paths. Whether or not that's true, we can agree that each person must decide what really matters in this world (and whatever is beyond), and then try to find a way to secure it.

Given our severe limitations, however—limitations of each person's time and place and experience and education and so on— we might wonder if the quest for certainty, especially about the ultimate questions of life and death, good and evil, the sacred and the secular, the eternal and the temporal, is doomed. Can we find genuine answers, or merely satisfy personal preferences? Is there any way to reliably apprehend and comprehend what is real?

I see a middle course between unjustifiable certainty and cynical despair. Philosophers sometimes call this general view "critical realism."[4] Human beings can know very little with certainty. Each of us, as limited and biased as we are, could well be wrong about almost anything we think we know. I believe, however, that God has given us intuition, imagination, reason, senses, memory, conscience, the heritage of the past, each other's company, and other good gifts to help us think about things. As we make (more or less) good use of these gifts, we run up against reality every day, and it needs explaining. The thoughtful person will try to find out what explains it best—all of it. Yes, we cannot help but view and conceive of the world through particular cognitive frameworks and basic convictions, through patterns of conscious and unconscious assumptions, impressions, and conclusions. We cannot see things purely objectively. But *we do see things*, and the best we can do is to keep refining our hypotheses—however particular, however general—to make the most sense we can of what we experience. So we can be *realistic* in the sense that we believe we have real experience of a real world, but we can also be conscious of at least some of what hinders and distorts our apprehension of the world, and so we ought to be *critically* realistic.

Furthermore, we should not reject an option merely because it cannot offer us perfect knowledge that answers all our questions to our complete satisfaction. No religion or philosophy—at least, none of the ones that have endured the test of time—even claims to do that. (Some weird cults might—and the very offer of "certain and comprehensive knowledge" is a telltale sign that you're in the vicinity of something suspicious.) So waiting until one has every doubt erased and every question answered is to wait for what will never arrive. Our real choice is among real options, and the wise person selects the best of those available. Then he goes on to live accordingly, all the while staying alert for opportunities to refine that option or even "trade up" to a significantly better alternative.

"Making sense of experience," let's be clear, is not limited to "figuring things out." It's not just a matter of assessing and then assenting to a particular set of ideas. At a profoundly basic level, the religious challenge also includes making an art of life. We want to construct our existence in beauty and integrity and fruitfulness and love. That's what we seek, and we should not be satisfied until we find it. Religions are about all of life, and they demand the allegiance of the whole person. In assessing them, therefore, we need to be both open and critical not only intellectually but also morally, aesthetically, emotionally, socially, and so on. Morally, for example, we must ask ourselves whether we are open to a new, better way of understanding what it means to live a good life, which would mean changing our behavior. Someone might tell us that denying the physical body in the interests of elevating the spirit is the best way to live. Another religion might ask us to surrender some of our autonomy to the group. Are we open to either of those options, at least a little? And are we also prepared to consider critically whether either view is both true and helpful?

Thinking about religion with the seriousness it deserves ultimately entails taking one's life in one's hands. One has to love the truth to find the truth. The most important things in life rarely come to those who do not press hard after them: not music, not literature, not athletic skills, not wholesome relationships. Religion is about the very deepest questions of our existence, so it offers the greatest challenge of venturesome thinking: of investigating, and weighing up, and living without certainty—and perhaps even living without a religious "home" for a while—as we decide. That's what it costs to adequately consider the most important decision one can ever make: the direction of one's life, and whatever life there is to come.

Suppose, then, we have come to some conclusions in our religious quest. Suppose we have decided upon a specific religious option. Where does religious commitment come in? What about faith?

Knowledge as a Condition for Faith—and Vice Versa

In the Christmas movie *Miracle on 34th Street*, a little girl wrestling with doubts about Santa Claus bravely recites her mother's wisdom: "Faith is believing when common sense tells you not to." However appropriate such a maxim might be with respect to the existence and identity of Kris Kringle, it may not immediately satisfy when it comes to faith in God. Folk wisdom about religious faith is even more problematic when chirped by the bright-eyed Sunday school pupil: "Faith is believing something you know isn't true!"[5]

Aristotle famously divided our ideas into three categories: opinion, belief, and knowledge—with religious conviction being located in the middle category.[6] Long before him, of course, religious thinkers wrestled with the question of how faith relates to knowledge. Is faith just a religious kind of knowledge? Is faith inferior to knowledge, or perhaps somehow superior to it? Are faith and knowledge utterly different from each other, and even opposed to each other?

Two mistakes typically show up in this context. The first is to think that faith is a peculiarly religious word and has nothing to do with everyday life. The second is to think that faith is a peculiarly religious word and has no relationship to knowledge. In fact, we exercise faith all the time and we place our faith in all sorts of things and people. Everyday life constantly presses us beyond what we know (or think we know) and requires us to exercise faith. We frequently find ourselves compelled to trust beyond what we're sure of, to take risks that lie outside our sense of complete assurance. We wait at the platform, a train rumbles in, and we get on. Do we know categorically that it is safe? No. Yet these moments of trust and commitment—these acts of faith—are not arbitrary leaps into the void, but are intrinsically and importantly related to knowledge.

Faith is what we do when we cantilever our lives out over what we do not and cannot know, while anchoring ourselves upon what we think we do know. Faith relies on knowledge even as it moves out from knowledge into the unknown. No one exercises "blind faith" in anything or anyone. Everyone has a reason to believe what he or she believes, even if someone else thinks it to be an insufficient reason, and even if that belief turns out to be a mistake.

This relationship of knowledge and faith holds in matters large and small, impersonal and personal. Life compels me to trust beyond what I know for sure. I would be a fool to refuse to sit in a chair until its adequacy had been conclusively demonstrated by a team of structural engineers. Parents of small children can never have an evening out if they refuse to trust any babysitter because they lack comprehensive knowledge of her entire life. Human life entails risk, and the wise person does not seek certainty but seeks instead *adequate* reason to believe—and to believe the best alternative available. Then, having satisfied herself that she can do so, she ventures forward in faith, trusting something or someone because of what she thinks she knows about that thing or person.

This doesn't always work out well, of course. I have faith in my ski instructor. I trust her to lead me to hills that will help me improve my skills but not imperil my life. Sadly, my faith in such instances has not always been well grounded and I have experienced a few breathless moments ruing my lack of due diligence in selecting a guide. We can acknowledge, furthermore, that there is a "gradient" to faith. I might trust you with a loan of ten dollars, but not know you well enough to trust you with ten thousand. Still, there is also an all-or-nothing, binary nature to faith. Trevor cannot know for certain that this canoe bobbing by the dock will still float once he gets in it, but there is no practical way for him to be "mostly convinced" and thus somehow place most of his weight in the canoe while reserving some of his weight for the dock. To experience the canoe, he has to get all the way in. If he tries instead to nicely distribute his body in strict proportion to his confidence in the canoe, he might straddle the two briefly but will soon find himself enjoying the benefits of neither canoe nor dock. He has to make a (full) commitment. The parents cannot enjoy their date night out if one or both of them are constantly phoning home to see how things are going—or glancing every five minutes at the nanny-cam feed on their phones. Every exercise of faith requires a kind of letting go.

We try to be as sure as we think we need to be in proportion to the risk we're going to run.

As dependent as faith is upon knowledge, so knowledge is dependent on faith. This book is being written during an era of "fake news," of widespread disbelief in the so-called mainstream media serving large portions of the American population. One cannot learn anything from the *New York Times* if one refuses to trust the *New York Times*—and that goes for Fox News or whatever news medium one prefers. The same is true in the world of social relationships. Carla is getting acquainted with a new boyfriend. If she assumes the worst, or keeps him at a skeptical arm's length indefinitely, she will learn only a little about him. Some initial skepticism is healthy and safe, of course. But if she cannot believe anything he says without corroboration of a legally adequate kind ("How do I know you really have the job you say you have? Do you have a pay stub to show me? Can I come to the place where you say you work and interrogate the other employees? How can I know that you're not a pimp or a bigamist? Can I hire a private detective to watch you for the next month?"), then most of us would pronounce the relationship doomed. She will never be satisfied as long as she has these extreme suspicions and these impossible standards of proof. Indeed, she can always twist the evidence to fit her dark fantasies.

Carla's lack of faith eventually will result in an end to new data forthcoming from her beau. At some point, he will recoil from her relentless doubts and decide not to reveal any more of himself to her. He will feel insulted, treated with less faith than he deserves, and will want nothing more to do with this woman who must decide on everything for herself. Carla will learn nothing more from him. That's what can happen in any personal relationship. The "investigated" party can choose whether or not to reveal more to the "investigator." And if the investigator fails to move forward in appropriate increments of faith in his colleague or her friend, then he or she risks losing the partnership or friendship under the crushing weight of the arrogant demand to know it all on one's own terms.

In many sorts of knowledge, therefore, ranging in these examples from the most objective to the most subjective, faith of an appropriate sort is necessary to learn and to understand. Far from being opposed, it turns out that faith and knowledge are in a dialectical relationship. These considerations and illustrations may have struck the patient reader as ranging pretty far from our topic of religion, but they haven't. Let's connect them explicitly now with religious faith, whatever that is.

Religious Faith

Religious faith is not completely different from the faith we have been discussing. Religious faith is simply the variety of faith proper to its object. Putting faith in a chair is similar to, though also different than, putting faith in a spouse. Likewise, putting faith in a deity, or several deities, or in a religion with no deities, is both similar to, and also somewhat different than, the other two exercises of faith. We expect to have different warrants for trusting a piece of furniture versus trusting a marriage partner. Likewise, the warrants will be different still for trusting the God of Christianity. This God is normally invisible to us, and so divine activity must be inferred from its results, or believed in on the basis of reliable testimony, while spouses perform a great many actions that we can readily observe. And chairs are, so to say, right there. Different stakes are involved in each relationship. We trust a chair with our bodies and a spouse with our lives, while we trust a deity to guide and provide for us reliably for eternity.

We therefore arrive at two crucial propositions about the quest for religious certainty: it is impossible, but it is also unnecessary. We already are accustomed to taking the greatest of relational risks in this life, whether trusting a romantic partner, a surgeon, or a rescuer on a mountain ledge. We must perform the same exercise of trust in religious matters as well, as human beings who recognize that we do not and cannot know it all before deciding—on any-thing. To return for a moment to our new friend Carla, she must commit to her marriage on her wedding day, yes, but also continue to exercise faith every succeeding day of her marriage. For she will never arrive at full knowledge either of her husband's character or of his activities when he is not in her presence. And we would nor-mally say that she is entirely right to keep trusting him—at least until the sad day, if it ever comes, when the warrants against contin-uing to trust him properly overwhelm her faith. Strange perfume on his shirt, unknown female callers on the phone, loss of affection when he is with her: such data eventually add up. Then, we would conclude, she must indeed change her mind, and her life, accord-ingly. Admirable faith is not willful and foolish blindness.

Having faith can never require the suspension of critical thinking. And faith doesn't mean irrationality, let alone stubborn-ness, in the religious sphere, either. You might be entirely entitled to believe in religion X given what you have learned in life to this point. But if you run up against challenges (what contemporary philosophers call "potential defeaters and underminers"), you are obliged to pay attention to them. You don't need to throw your faith aside at the first sign of trouble. That would be as silly as a scientist trashing years of research whenever a lab result came up "wrong," or Carla dumping her husband the first time he seems to hedge about what he did on his business trip. The truly respon-sible person, however, pays attention to such difficulties. She tries creatively to see if they can be accommodated within her current scheme of thought, or whether she needs to modify her views a bit, or—in the extreme case—whether she needs to abandon her theory (about this chemical process, about this spouse, or about this reli-gion) for a better one.

We thus face the crucial question: Can I believe? This book, and any book, can provide at best only intellectual warrants and suggestions for further investigation. Those warrants, in turn, can provide at best only reasonable support for faith. They cannot prove the truth of Christianity (or any other religion) beyond a reasonable doubt, since (a) some of the most basic matters discussed in most religions are profound beyond any total explanation, let alone complete proof; (b) most of us don't have the expertise to assess the finer points of such matters; (c) other religions with different claims offer their own warrants that deserve respectful acknowledgment; and (d) we each are influenced by what we perceive to be in our own interest to believe is the truth. As philosopher Alvin Plantinga warns, "In religious belief as elsewhere, we must take our chances, recognizing that we could be wrong, dreadfully wrong. There are no guarantees; the religious life is a venture; foolish and debilitating error is a permanent possibility."[7]

Christian thinkers at least as far back as Blaise Pascal warn us that demands for proof may amount to attempts to obviate the requirement of faith, the requirement to trust God as a dependent rather than pass judgment on God as a superior. The most important lesson God has to teach us is that God is God and we are not—that our whole welfare rests on God and so we badly, basically need God. This lesson is the unlearning of our fundamental human mistake: to decide and do entirely for ourselves, rather than to trust God to guide and provide. Craig Gay writes, "It is for this reason that it would be pointless—and even counterproductive—for God to reveal himself too unambiguously at present. The interests of genuine faith and trust would simply not be served in the provocation of grudging submission."[8] Being crushed by overwhelming force isn't the most promising posture from which to develop a loving, grateful relationship.

The best one can hope for is to find warrant sufficient to believe—which is precisely, let's remember, all one can properly ask for in any other exercise of faith. So if we're considering the Christian faith, or any other claim to Explain It All, there had better be a *lot* of evidence, and of the right sort, to justify trusting our lives to it in this world and whatever is beyond.

But before we consider that explanation (which is the next major section of this book) and the grounds Christians have to trust it (which comes after that), we need to put together in summary fashion what we have discussed so far, and then add a few nuances, before we're quite done.

How to Decide about Religion

Deciding about religion is like deciding about anything else. You consider a "live option," marshal what you take to be the relevant evidence and most potent contrary arguments, deliberate upon it all, and decide whether to adopt, adapt, or abandon that option.

This picture of knowledge, however, is too simple. Knowing in any complex sphere of thought is not a straight-line inference from data to conclusion. Instead, our thinking is always dialectical, a to-and-fro between information and interpretation. Most of what most of us read most of the time we can take in at a glance, or without much thought, and certainly without multiple readings. But serious intellectual work on difficult matters requires more effort. We have an initial impression of Shakespeare's *Hamlet*, formed from flotsam and jetsam we've encountered in popular culture and family conversation. But then we see it performed well, and we form a much richer interpretation. From there, we might read the play, consult critics and historians about it, view other performances of it—and each experience not only enriches but in some ways alters, or even corrects, our previous interpretation.

The rich parts of our lives—such as getting to (really) know other people, and especially our significant others—are like this as well. So are politics, and art, and the other important themes of life. We come at them with some kind of pre-understanding; we then encounter them in a succession of experiences of particular bits and pieces; and we thus confirm, modify, or replace our general understanding of the subject. We then, if we choose to do so, carry on into further experiences, which feed back into our general understanding.

If we are circumspect, therefore, we do not claim to have arrived at the endpoint of any serious matter. We do not think of ourselves as having comprehended all the information there is to know and to have inferred from it indubitable conclusions of timeless truth. If we are appropriately modest, we think of our conception as "the best hypothesis so far," one that is by definition open to revision, if not in fact replacement, as new data or interpretative options occur to us. This openness is what keeps us from fanaticism, from the conviction that we are absolutely right and that nothing could possibly arise to alter our view.

To be sure, on various matters we might be very, very, very confident. A first-year philosophy student home for Thanksgiving dinner decides to provoke us with "How do you know you're really a man dreaming he's a butterfly, rather than a butterfly dreaming he's a man?" We might smile indulgently and reply, "I don't know with certainty that I am not a butterfly. But I have no good reason to suspect I am a butterfly, and every good reason I can think of to believe I am a man. Please pass the gravy." We spend precisely zero minutes that weekend wracked with existential doubt. Yet, at least theoretically, we remain open to alternatives, since we do not claim to be omniscient. Thus the holiday can pass without shouting, at least over epistemology.

Religious knowledge is like that. We search for the best hypothesis we can find to explain the information we think is pertinent, all the while remaining, at least theoretically, open to new data and new ways of seeing the data. Thinking in these terms lets us do what we're going to do in this book—namely, to start with a particular hypothesis (Christianity) and set out the grounds for its credibility. We can start anywhere we like—with intriguing data or with attractive hypotheses, it doesn't matter which—so long as we then go back and forth between information and interpretation to assess whether the idea we have in our hands is clear, coherent, correct, comprehensive, and cogent. Having assessed its positive grounds, we can then assail it with the best arguments we can find against it. And if it can pass those tests, we compare how well it passed against any rival options we think worth considering. What emerges from this gauntlet is then what we believe—at least until we have reason to reconsider.[9]

Even this picture of how we think about anything, and about religion in particular, requires a little more qualification—for such "hermeneutical spirals" are not guaranteed to proceed in positive directions. One's thinking can, in fact, get steadily worse. Originally, I thought Keith was a nice enough fellow, but then he seemed to interfere with my work, and now I'm quite convinced he's out to get me. Psychologists would warn me, of course, about one or another of the dozens of cognitive difficulties that might incline me to an increasingly incorrect view of the situation and of my workmate—problems such as "confirmation bias" and "attribution bias" and "paranoia" and so on. We tend to see what we want—or expect—to see, and we tend to believe to be true what confirms what we already believe to be true. We tend to interpret the world in our favor, so to speak, and against those we judge to be our enemies. I'm big, you're fat, and my enemy is morbidly obese—even though our body mass indexes are exactly the same.

Such interpretative problems are compounded by social facts. In my late teens I lived and worked for a while in West Texas. There was much to like and admire about that culture, but the easy racism was startling to me as a transplant from northern Canada. My supervisors seemed like good men—church deacons and Sunday school teachers, some of them—and they treated me with patience and good humor. But they also traded constantly in racist jokes— perhaps even more than usual, since there was what they called a "Canadian Yankee" among them whom they liked to tease. Clearly they lived in a white community of constantly and easily reinforced attitudes toward blacks and Hispanics.

What was more insidious about the situation is that this white community so dominated life in West Texas that most of the non-white people who could possibly leave had left. Thus the reinforcement of bias was realized in the actual experience of these white folks. They had literally never met a well-educated black person or Mexican, nor one in a position of professional authority. Their prejudice literally altered the cognitive environment to remove contradictory data. The hermeneutical spiral can bend away from the truth, rather than toward it, if sufficiently interfered with by our preferences.

We therefore have to take stock of the moral and social fact that our thinking about things is usually deeply affected by our interests, our hopes and fears, our longings and frustrations, our values, and our social situation. What, if anything, can we do about this dark fact?

First, we can pick our company. I tell my undergraduate students, "If you want to get smarter, get smarter friends." We tend to resemble our peers, so we should select those peers to help us make good decisions. In the case of religion, we can hardly expect to think straight about Mormonism if we converse only with bitter ex-Mormons or hardened religious skeptics. We can hardly expect to fairly consider Hinduism in the company only of fervent Christian converts from India who now think of Hinduism entirely and only in terms of dark idols in darkened temples dispensing darker magic. If we're going to take a religious option seriously, we need to be among people who practice that religious option seriously—or at least spend a proper amount of time among such people so that the initial implausibility produced by sheer strangeness can wear off and proper investigation of the religion can proceed.

Second, we can widen the conversation to include people we can count on to see things differently from us and our peer group. If you're a man, find out what women think. If you're older, talk to younger people. If you're middle-class, listen to those who aren't. Diversity of viewpoint can only help you round out your view of things, and perhaps even bring to light positive or negative information otherwise unobtainable to those with your vantage point. At some time, in fact, you should even listen to those ex-Mormons or ex-Hindus to see what they have to offer your thinking. Before making up your mind, you need to subject your hypotheses to the most searching antagonists you can find. Only then can your confidence be justified.

In fact, including people who don't think as we do is vital to another crucial aspect of thought: imagination. We all ignore options we judge to be implausible—not worth taking seriously. Life is short, and busy, and none of us can, or should, give equal time to every possible alternative whenever we think about something. We are therefore limited not only by our particular stores of information (what we know) and our particular reasoning abilities (what we can conclude from what we know), but also by our imaginations (what we can imagine might be true from what we know). Imagination is the crucial middle mode between intuition (apprehending things) and reason (deciding about things). Søren Kierkegaard famously argued that the decline of faith among his contemporary nineteenth-century European intellectuals was not primarily a result of their encountering facts or theories that undermined Christianity. Their apostasy was the result of a shrinking mental world, a steady reduction of what was thinkable to the plane of the material and quotidian, under the impressive prestige of natural science and technology. Encountering indisputably admirable believers helps us to widen the windows of our minds to at least consider alternatives that might be illuminating. Heeding the experiences of such people might keep us from uttering pronouncements such as, "I just can't imagine a God who would . . . ," as if they are statements about the universe when they are simply admissions about the boundaries of our imaginations.

Finally, we can acknowledge the role of the will in our believing. Deciding among various understandings of God and the world is not merely a matter of the intellect: "Let's add up the arguments and evidence in columns A, B, and C and calculate which religious option comes out best." Deciding about religious faith goes beyond analysis by the intellect to action by the will.

When it comes to most intellectual matters, to be sure, it seems that the will is irrelevant. One does not "choose" to believe something. One is either convinced by its warrants or not—or, in most instances, we would profess to be *more or less* convinced by the warrants at hand. When I lecture on these subjects, I sometimes raise my hand and offer members of the audience a million dollars to believe that I am holding up in front of them a bright blue parrot when I am in fact merely dangling my car keys. Some people just laugh, but others scrunch up their faces, seem to turn on their imaginations full blast, and apparently really try to believe I am holding a parrot. But try as they might to believe in that parrot, they simply can't. We *are convinced*—we cannot *choose* to be convinced.

Some important elements of rationality, however, are indeed subject to our wills. We can decide which sources of information to investigate, and how thoroughly we will search. We can decide whether, and how seriously, to consider alternative points of view. We can decide whether to ask hard questions of our motives—or others'—and so on. To a considerable extent, in fact, our wills affect our thinking. At the last, though, we cannot help but believe what we think are the best-warranted concepts and to trust in what we think the evidence shows are the most reliable people.

If we grant that the will doesn't have much to do once it comes time to actually decide about intellectual matters, the will nonetheless is clearly and importantly operative in every human decision to *trust* rather than merely to *conclude*. One finally has to decide whether to get in that canoe, or leave one's children with the sitter, or sign on the dotted line with one's partner—or commit oneself to this or that religion. To commit oneself body and soul to someone or something need not require certainty—in the strict sense of "knowing I am right about this and knowing, furthermore, that I could not possibly be wrong." And it's a good thing, too, since the act of faith is by definition going beyond what we think we know "for sure." But we can *commit ourselves* to a cause, or a person, or a deity without holding anything back. We follow that particular road the best we can, moment by moment, day by day, until it gets us where we want to go—or turns out to be a false trail. That's all we can do. We can't walk on two or more paths at once, but on only one at a time, however confident we may feel about this route. And we cannot walk any such path without willing at each moment to take each step—a step of faith.

The will figures in religious decisions in a more specific way, according to Christian doctrine. As we see in more detail in the chapters that follow, the fundamental human problem, according to the Christian explanation of things, is not ignorance (a deficiency in the intellect), or deprivation (a deficiency in our environment), but sin (a defect in the soul). We are, in some important sense, alienated from God, even resistant toward God. God, after all, does cramp our style, limit our autonomy, humble our pride, and restrict our freedom—and who likes that?

We might nonetheless think that we would gladly choose the right path if God would just make things obvious, especially if God became visible and spoke to us audibly. You yourself might not think this way, but you may have had conversations with people who claimed that if God would just give them a sign, a miracle, an indubitable proof of the divine presence, they would believe. And, they imply, until God comes across this way, they will not believe.

According to the Hebrew Bible, however, a whole generation of Israelites experienced God's local and tangible presence in the wilderness after the great escape from slavery in Egypt. Not only did they witness the thunder and lightning of Mount Sinai, but as they traveled on from there, God was right in their midst, in the "tent of meeting." Moses would go in to consult with God "as a man speaks with his friend" (Exodus 33:11). With all of these warrants, did these witnesses to the presence of God therefore become especially devout?

On the contrary. They proved to be whiny, greedy, impatient, and disobedient brats who kept demanding that God perform *now* according to their immediate whims or they would huffily march back to Egypt. God's dramatic revelation of his existence, power, and goodness was apparently no guarantee of ongoing faith, much less of spiritual goodness or wisdom. God's evident proximity was not the solution. It only made more obvious the real source of trouble: the hearts of the people themselves. So God had to wait them out and bring the next generation into the Promised Land instead. And if we aren't convinced by this story from the Old Testament, we might consider how people responded in the New Testament when, as Christians believe, God took human form and lived among us for several decades in the person of Jesus Christ. That story, full of miracles performed in public, had a dreadfully unhappy ending.

No, the problem—again, from a Christian point of view— is rarely that God is far away. I say "rarely" because I respect the "dark night of the soul," a sense of divine abandonment reported by believers at least as far back as the Psalms and as recently as Mother Teresa. But these experiences are generally reported by advanced spiritual practitioners.[10] The problem for most of us, most of the time, is what we tend to do with God. And before we're done, we'll have to address again this problem of the will in believing.

Are we getting ahead of ourselves, however, with all this talk of Exodus and Moses and Jesus? Perhaps. But it's worth remembering once more as we set out together that we should check our attitude and remember the influence of our wills, not just our minds. I wouldn't be a good guide if I didn't ask, Will we truly make ourselves open to considering things differently? Or are we getting ready to go to "red alert" at the first sign of something challenging?

We need to see the question of religion as a matter of discovery, not of choice. Religions purport to be explanations of reality, maps to the (ultimately) real world. It would be perverse to say, "Well, I concede that your map seems much more accurate. Still, I prefer mine because it makes me feel better about myself as it shows me to have made much more progress than your map indicates." Deciding about religion has to be about what is true, not about what I wish. So let's see what the world's most popular Map of Everything has to say.

2

What Is Christianity?

Introduction: A Fourfold Scheme

For more than twenty years, I have been introducing students to the major religions of the world. And I have had the opportunity to discuss the tenets of Christianity in comparison with other religions in a fairly wide range of contexts—in inter-religious discussions at Yale and Stanford Universities; in conferences in Israel, Malaysia, and India; and in classrooms in Korea, Australia, and the United Kingdom.

Because I am not an academic expert on any religion other than Christianity, I have found it helpful as both a student and a teacher of other religions to work with heuristics—helpful mental tools to organize what can be intimidatingly complex phenomena. One commonly used heuristic to get at the essence of a religion is this series of four questions: What is the ultimate nature of the cosmos? What is the best we can hope for? Why don't we enjoy it? What can we do about that gap?

In short: What's real? What's best? What's wrong? And what can be done?

When I was lecturing in China (at Fudan, Wuhan, and Hong Kong Universities), this fourfold heuristic helped me introduce Christianity to audiences much more familiar with Buddhism, Confucianism, Daoism, and communism. Let's use the first of these to illustrate the heuristic.

What is traditionally understood to be the earliest form of Buddhism, the Theravada strand ("Theravada" means "tradition of the elders"), answers the four questions like this: The world is an endless wheel of suffering, because no matter how luxurious your life might be, eventually some combination of poverty, sickness, and finally death will rob you of all its pleasures and bring you only disappointment, loss, and pain. And then it all starts up again in a next life because your attachment to this world keeps you stuck on the wheel of rebirth (the wheel that is assumed by all major Indian religions). If you possibly can, therefore, you want to get off this wheel. The most fundamental problem here, for Buddhism, is our desire. We quest after what we don't have and we cling to what we do have, while life inevitably prevents us from realizing all our dreams even as it finally pries whatever we have accomplished out of our dead hands. Since we cannot get all we want and we cannot keep what we do get, we face a never-ending round of suffering: of fear, frustration, loss, and pain. There is no alternative "happy place" in which we can be endlessly happy. The best we can hope for, taught the Buddha, is to stop suffering. If you can't gain all that you want, and you can't keep all that you gain, the best thing possible is: stop wanting. You can't suffer if you don't care. Cessation of desire lets us detach ourselves from this pain-ridden existence and stop existing. *Nirvana*, the goal of Buddhist aspiration, is "where the candle flame goes when the candle stops burning," as the Buddha told one of his followers. ("Nirvana" literally means "to blow out" or "to quench.") This relinquishment of desire and, indeed, of being is the supreme good in Theravada Buddhism.

Note that this non-being is not the best state *one might imagine*. Anyone can imagine an eternal paradise superior to this empty blank of non-suffering. But enlightened ones see things as they really are. They are those for whom the light of the truth has been switched on, so to speak, so that they clearly perceive what is hidden from the rest of us. (*Bodhi* means "enlightenment," from which the title *buddha* comes.) Enlightened ones know that such everlasting vacations are not on offer from the universe. The best state that is *actually available* to human beings is this (non-)state of non-being.

To help my North American students connect with what to most is a strange idea, I remind them that if one has loved and lost, one can feel as if one wants never to love again. The pain is too great, it seems, to justify whatever pleasure came from the now-ruptured relationship. This instinct to avoid pain is powerful within us—some psychologists suggest it is at least twice as strong as the instinct to obtain pleasure.[1] Theravada Buddhism arises out of this fundamental human disposition. One can avoid all suffering by detaching from all that causes it, which is—all.

What can be done to achieve this detachment? Buddhism teaches the Noble Eightfold Path—ranging from initial insight as to the way things truly are ("right view") to final release ("right consciousness"). The Buddhist tradition offers three major helps: the example of the Buddha, the teachings of Buddhism, and the Buddhist community. One makes good use of these resources and eventually (perhaps only after several more reincarnations) one can finally detach.

Any religion or philosophy, any *functional* religion, can be analyzed according to this fourfold scheme, and we'll use it to outline the Christian religion. But just before we do, we need to begin an important process—namely, to make Christianity strange again.

The Strangeness of Christianity

Whenever I teach introductory surveys of world religions to university students, I always dread discussing the same two religions.

One is Hinduism. Hinduism is fascinating, but it is enormously difficult to introduce to students. Indeed, it's not at all clear that there is such a thing as Hinduism. For some time now, scholars have suggested that the term "Hinduism" was invented for the conceptual convenience of European traders and then British colonial administrators in India. It was a catch-all for the bewildering array of religions they encountered in that vast land that were *not*

Buddhism, Jainism, Sikhism, Islam, Christianity, or some other more clearly identifiable religion. Everything else was grouped together under the category of "Indian religion"—which is what "Hinduism" actually means: the "ism" of the people who live near the Indus River (from the ancient Greeks and Persians who originated the "Hindu" word group).

When I first was tasked as a junior professor with teaching a course on world religions, I encountered endless frustration in trying to execute the basic responsibility of any introductory guide: reducing complexity to simplicity. I read book after book, seeking a convenient list of generalizations that would help students quickly understand the essence of Hinduism so as to distinguish it from other religions, especially the somewhat similar traditions of Buddhism and Jainism. But I kept encountering forms of Hinduism, often quite popular forms, that defied whatever generalization I was formulating.

At last, I left my office and walked down the hall to visit my department head, who was, conveniently enough, a world-class expert on Hinduism. I confessed my frustration to him and received in return one of his rare smiles. "Ah," he said. "You're catching on."

As I digested this double-edged affirmation, he went on. "Besides the karma-dharma cycle that is basic to all Indian religions, there are only two distinguishing characteristics of all Hindu varieties."

Only two? I thought. It will be hard to build a lecture series on only two.

"First, respect for the Vedas," the most ancient layer of Hindu Scriptures, dating back to about 1500 BC. All forms of Hinduism trace their lineage back to the Vedas—however much their teachings might seem, to others, to diverge from them—while Buddhism and Jainism, by contrast, have their own scriptures and pay no attention to the Vedas.

So far, so good. What is the other common trait?

"Second, respect for the social hierarchy as timelessly valid." My colleague meant that Hinduism of every sort takes for granted, and usually teaches explicitly, the complex layers of the famous Indian caste system in which one's daily life is governed by one's inherited social position, from which one must not attempt to stray on pain of incurring bad karma and being reincarnated in an even lower state. And that was that. Everything else was up for grabs, it seemed. To be sure, there are other generalizations that can helpfully be made about Indian religion.[2] But still, one must be careful to constantly say "most" or "some" or "almost all" or "hardly any" when discussing Hinduism, which is tiresome for teacher and student alike. So teaching Hinduism is no treat.

The other religion I dreaded to introduce to beginning students, however, was Christianity. The problem here was not that Christians disagree with each other so much. Yes, one reliable estimate puts the number of Christian denominations (= "formally named varieties") in the world at about forty-five thousand.[3] But Christians do, in fact, share a distinguishable nucleus of shared tenets and practices. It can seem as if there isn't much in common among Roman Catholic, Pentecostal, and Amish believers, but every university-level textbook I have encountered agrees that Christianity teaches a common core of doctrine and practices, a common array of rituals and morals, according to a common set of values. That's why I can hope to summarize Christianity helpfully in this brief book.

No, the problem is not Christian diversity, formidable as it is. The problem is that in the very heart of Christian beliefs, practices, and values there are some very strange elements. Because of the global extension of Western culture through mass media, tourism, and so on, terms such as "Trinity" and "Incarnation" and "Atonement" may elicit at least a nod of acquaintance from most readers of this book, as they will from many people around the world. Yet this superficial familiarity masks two crucial realities. Most people, even believers, would be hard-pressed to provide a theologically correct definition of these ideas. And, once they got started trying to articulate them, they would pretty quickly realize how very odd

Christian teachings are, conventional as they have seemed because of this slight familiarity.

Most of the religions that have lasted—the ones that, in competition with tribal religions and large-scale (or "world") religions in the vicinity, have gained large followings—make claims that seem convincing to large numbers of people. But isn't that a truism? Ipso facto the popular religions are the ones that make claims that are popularly convincing. What I'm getting at here—and I say this with great respect—is that these broadly convincing religions teach things that, if properly understood, seem sensible to teach. They are the sorts of Big Explanations that, when encountered with some sympathetic imagination and intelligent attentiveness, one could respond to with, "Yes, as strange as I first thought that was, I can see it now. I can understand why people would find that explanation of things compelling."

Theravada Buddhism, austere as it is, makes sense to anyone who has experienced great disappointment. If we turn for a moment to Islam, a very different religion, we find that it is also, at its foundation, a simple and coherent set of ideas. Rich as Islamic tradition has become in so many respects, from philosophy to art, the core of Islam is clear: one God, one keyscripture, and one definitive prophet and exemplar that together articulate a scheme of morality and devotion according to which there will be appropriate rewards and punishments easily imaginable in an afterlife of either a paradisiacal oasis or a horrific fire. Even allowing for the sometimes grim realities of Islamic imperialism and the differences among various forms of Islam around the globe, it is no wonder Islam has spread so far and so fast, gaining so many apparently sincere believers. It readily makes sense.

So does the social philosophy of Confucianism, and so do the individual-focused ethics of Daoism and Stoicism. The most popular form of Hinduism, *bhakti* (devotional Hinduism), marries the straightforward "if this, then that" logic of the karma-dharma worldview (if you do your duty, your *dharma*, you are performing good actions—*karma*—which will conduce to your moving upward when you are reincarnated; and if you don't, you'll move down, in exact proportion to your deeds) with the hope of assistance from a divinity (hence the prayers rendered to the various Hindu deities). Even if one finds the welter of Hindu myths disorienting or even discomfiting, one can fairly quickly see why so many people would hold to this basic way of negotiating the world.[4]

Christianity, for all its global popularity in the modern world, and for all its familiarity to most readers of this book, is by comparison strange—*extremely* strange.[5]

To be sure, popular versions of Christianity aren't all that strange. Indeed, they have become popular precisely by reducing the scandals of traditional Christian teachings to anodyne principles of general metaphysics and morality.[6] Think of what has happened to Christmas. According to the Bible, the center of the Christmas Story is that the Jewish deity, Yhwh, somehow literally becomes a human infant in order to grow up to accomplish several huge tasks: provide a model of what it means to live as a renewed human being; teach everyone the definitive truth about God, the world, and everything; and suffer, die, and rise again from the grave in a way that secures the salvation of all humanity. That is why the baby in the manger is to be named "Jesus" (literally "Yhwh saves!"), for "he will save his people from their sins" (Matthew 1:21). Now, how much of that very surprising, very particular, very *central* content shows up in the holiday television specials, the mall decorations, and the elevator music of Yuletide? Not much. Instead, we are told, year after year, that Christmas is "all about" some general, inoffensive sentiment: love, generosity, forgiveness, renewal, hope, and so on and so forth. Who doesn't believe in those things? Who, in fact, needs Christmas to celebrate them? The preposterous doctrines of Christmas are thus reduced, quite drastically, to what most of us can pretty readily believe.

Likewise, some forms of popular religion trade in health-and-wealth promises, or the promotion of self-esteem, or the welcoming of everyone and every idea, or the bolstering of national pride, or the preservation of middle-class respectability, or the production of vague but powerful spiritual experiences—onto which religious entrepreneurs can stick a cross or a fish and market it as Christianity. But such generic alternatives find little support in any serious reading of the Bible.[7]

So what does the Bible actually say? The answer ought to surprise you, since it is, as I say, extremely strange. Two features of this odd narrative might impress you, as they have so many others. First, its various elements, bizarre as they might be individually, cohere into an account that, on its own terms, makes sense. That utterly strange figure at the center of the Christian religion—the Man on the Cross—becomes intelligible, even inevitable, once you understand the backstory and, indeed, the story that follows as well.

The second striking feature of this odd narrative is that its elements not only cohere with each other but also correspond to the world as we experience it. As strange as the Christian Story is, the world is also strange, and with a like strangeness. And that is the reason, I argue here, why Christianity is the globe's most popular Explanation of Everything: because it seems—to those couple of billion people, anyway—to be the truth.

Let's take a closer look.

What Is Real: Creation

"In the beginning, God created the heavens and the earth." Those famous first words of the Bible pack multiple punches. Let's take a few of them in turn—although just before we do, let me note that the genre of early Genesis, and thus its implications for issues of history and science—particularly paleontology—is a vexed issue, of course. For our present purposes, however, all that matters is the theology of it, its teaching about God and God's purposes in creation. Just how literally we are to take the details is, again, an important issue in some discourses, but here we're focusing on the general religious teaching of the text. Readers interested in those other questions can find help in the sources listed in the notes.[8]

"In the beginning" asserts that there was, indeed, a beginning—to *this* cosmos. The Book of Genesis, after all, is a book addressed to humans who live in this particular universe, so its narrative describes this situation. Are there, or were there, other universes? Maybe. The Bible doesn't talk about that question. Is there a realm beyond this universe? Apparently: God existed before God made this universe. So, since the Bible doesn't declare that the universe is all that is, and even hints that there is more than this particular cosmos, we are free to investigate and speculate on that score.

What the Bible does say, however, is that there was a beginning to this cosmos, and that God initiated it: "God created the heavens and the earth." The universe is *intended*. The Deity—whom the early audience for the Book of Genesis would already know as Israel's God, the loving, powerful Lord of Mount Sinai who bested the Egyptians in delivering God's people from slavery and brought them to the Promised Land—this holy, wise, deliberate, and compassionate God is the Cause of the cosmos. The universe is thus no accident, but a project. However it came to be and progressed into its current shape, it is an *artifact* of the Supreme Being.[9] It therefore is laden with *purpose* and *value*—and purpose and value consistent with the character of its Maker.

The world is not, therefore, what it appears to be in some other religions: a farm to feed the gods, a torture chamber for the perverse amusement of decadent divinities, a material prison incarcerating spiritual sparks of the divine light, an illusion from which we must be awakened, or a testing ground to prove the worthiness of the victorious. The world is instead a *home*, a living environment made for the profusion and propagation of creatures and creativity.

Genesis 1 makes clear that the world is *designed*. God proceeds in an orderly fashion to construct a *habitat*—for the goal of his project is a world teeming with living things, from denizens of the deep to high-flying birds and everything in between. And these living things are commanded by this creative God to be (pro-)creative themselves—to reproduce and thus extend themselves over the whole earth (Genesis 1:22).

Humanity is created last as a special case. Indeed, unlike other stories ancient and modern, human beings are viewed in this story as special: truly earthly, of course, but not just another species, not merely one more type of entity in a blurry swarm under the gimlet eyes of the gods or of the stony stare of Being-in-General. Human dignity emerges here, in ancient Israel, as the creation of the Creator.[10]

In this story, God says that this last creature will be specially like God, created in God's very image (Genesis 1:26). And while the history of theology has attributed a dozen different explanations for what "the image of God" is, the most immediate interpretation has to be that the Creator, who has been creating throughout this passage, creates a creature who will thus be—creative. And, indeed, that's what God explicitly orders this new human pair to do: "Be fruitful, and multiply, and fill the earth, and subdue it." Be procreative—fan out over the world through your offspring—in order to subdue the world (Genesis 1:28).

But just a second. "Subdue" is a jarring imperative here. Isn't the world God created pronounced "very good"? So why does it need supervision, let alone subduing? Yes, it is created "very good"—but not *perfect*. The world is created young, full of potential. It is not created old, mature, fully realized—which is what ancient Hebrew means by "perfect." And, young as it is, the world needs taming. (I am not suggesting that the Bible teaches a "young earth" as in so-called creation science. Genesis depicts the youthful *quality* of the new creation, not the *quantity* of time it took to produce the world.)

This very good world is nonetheless *wild*. So God creates gardeners for it: "to till it and keep it" (Genesis 2:15), and to exercise constant care for it—to "have dominion over it" (1:28).

Uh-oh. There's another jarring word. "Dominion" sounds like "domination." But the word is derived from *dominus*, "lord," and here it means simply that human beings are to be the lords *created in the image of the Lord and acting as such.* So there is nothing here of exploitation. The human lords are to care for the world in the same way in which the divine Lord cares for all of us: generously, kindly, patiently, compassionately.

The basic Biblical picture of the world, then, is of a progressively cultivated garden within which and on behalf of which human beings engage in culture—from agriculture to all other forms of culture (metalworking and music show up early: Genesis 4). These "little lords" of the earth are created from the earth itself (2:7), and thus we remain in a symbiotic relationship with the rest of creation, our welfare bound up with the welfare of our fellow creatures. (Ecological thinking, contrary to the myth that "Christianity justifies the ruthless abuse of the earth," is fundamental to the Christian worldview.)[11] And over this global flourishing presides the one God.

The creation stories in Genesis are quite stark in comparison with the luxuriant myths typical of the ancient Near East. In Genesis there are not multiple deities vying for power or affection, but one God—such that God, in this narrative, needs no proper name to be identified among a pantheon. The usual candidates for godhood—sun and moon—are mere "lights" God puts in the sky as sources of illumination, nothing more. The great beasts of land and sea are just animals among the rest. The sea itself, daunting symbol of chaos to the landlocked Hebrews, is just so much water whose boundaries God has set, and thus is firmly under God's effortless control.[12]

And it *is* effortless. Rather than creation by combat or procreation, the usual methods by which gods are said to make the world, this God does literally the least possible: God merely speaks. I suppose God could do even less: merely think. But then we would have no divine action at all in the story. So God is shown as creating by fiat. In Genesis 1, God doesn't lift a finger, so to speak, to make the entire cosmos. (God seems to fashion humanity specially in the second story, Genesis 2:7, rather like a clay figurine, but even then it's not obvious how God does so.) That's how easy it all is for God, and how much everything depends on the will, the word, of God.

This Arcadian idyll serves as the initial model for a properly functioning world. Christian metaphysics includes the spiritual and the material in happy interaction within a single, integrated cosmos. There is no privileging of either over the other. The rest of the Biblical narrative unfolds a universe in which God, angels, demons, and humans interact with each other and with the natural world.

The Garden of Eden is not the once and future destiny of human beings. Despite a minority tradition in Christian thought that sees the end of human history curving back to a "peaceable kingdom" of bucolic serenity, the End of the World—both in the sense of "termination of this chapter of human existence" and "the purpose for which the world was created"—is not a garden, but a garden city.

What Is Best: Shalom

The greatest word in ancient Hebrew surely would be the very name of God: "Yhwh" (all consonants, since ancient Hebrew lacks vowels, and thus often spelled out with some added vowels as "Yahweh"). It is the name God told Moses to use when introducing God to the Egyptian pharaoh—a man surrounded by dozens of gods—as the deity who would rescue the enslaved Hebrews (Exodus 3:14).

The next greatest Hebrew word, however, is probably *shalom*. It is the word at the center of the Biblical hope for all creation. Literally translated as "peace," shalom is so much more than "the absence of conflict or noise," as in "peace and quiet." The closest English equivalent is probably *flourishing*—and in the widest, most inclusive sense.[13]

In the state of shalom, each individual has developed into its mature self. Potential is realized: seeds have become plants, infants have become adults, and the morally unstable have become rocks of solid virtue. Shalom also entails a flourishing relationship between each pair or group of individuals: husband and wife, parent and child, siblings, in-laws, friends, neighbors, workmates, even rivals. Shalom takes in groups, companies, and institutions. Now each business flourishes, and so does each hospital, university, government department, charity, musical ensemble, dance troupe, and utility. Shalom, then, means that each of these corporations treats each individual it encounters in the best possible way: employees, yes, but also customers, vendors, and regulators. Moreover, each group enjoys a flourishing relationship with every other group: government agencies with businesses and activist organizations alike, while schools get along well with parent groups and caterers and unions and boards. Shalom prompts all of these human beings, singly and together, to treat the rest of creation so as to promote the flourishing of each and all—from animals to plants to soils to waters to air. And this entire planet then basks in a flourishing relationship with God—not only individual humans at their prayers and each flower as it blossoms, but every organization, every nation, and every ecosystem cooperating fully, freely, and joyfully with each other and with God. Shalom, therefore, means *global flourishing*.

The Bible doesn't provide us with much detail about this world to come, this extension of all that is good about our current age into the next age of renewal and maturity, true *perfection* as the Bible means perfection. No classical ideal of frozen, geometric beauty, perfection, *shalom*, is a Middle Eastern idea of happiness and busyness, good company in worthy work, and raucous recreation and bountiful refreshment. The most detailed vision given in the Hebrew Bible is of a restored and lovely Jerusalem (Ezekiel 40–48— although it is never actually called "Jerusalem"), and in the New Testament it is transformed into a New Jerusalem of stupendous dimensions: a cubic city (yes, you read that right) measuring fifteen hundred miles on each side. This glorious city features the best things of this life improved to the horizon of imagination. The so-called pearly gates are single pearls so large they can function as entrances—through which one could, presumably, drive a vehicle. And the streets of gold are obviously not paved that way for optimal use (gold being a notoriously soft metal) but are pictured as such to convey the idea that the most precious things in our era are mere *construction materials* in the next.

   It is a city, yes, with all that that means in terms of work and leisure, culture and civilization, crowds as well as individuals—but it is a *garden* city. A river runs through it—which, as a Canadian, I find to be no big deal, but those from the desiccated Middle East would see such a feature to be the luxury of only great, privileged cities, along whose banks trees bear fruit *every season*—again, a literary flourish meant to indicate super-abundance, the best conceivable situation. (Our supermarkets at the ends of global trade routes largely remove from us the *seasonality* of fruit, the ancient world's single and always transitory source of sweetness. Imagine getting it all year round!—*that's* the wonder of these ever-fruiting trees.) It is a city constantly illuminated, and therefore free of the dark dangers of urban life, illuminated by the very presence of God, a symbol of everyone constantly communing with the Almighty in every sector of life—not just priestly elites in temples on high holy days bowing before sacred candles. "And there is no more sea" (Revelation 21:1). As a longtime inhabitant of Vancouver, I find this an odd promise, since the ocean provides us with so much joy. The ancient Hebrews, however, viewed the sea only as a terror, as the very embodiment of disordered menace; the idea here is that God has finally stilled all chaos.

   If we step back a moment, we can consider what this vision of the best life is *not*. It is not a distant spiritual realm filled with cottony clouds and harps of gold—the heaven we have been trained to believe in by centuries of Christian art strongly tinged by classical

Greek ideals of a timeless spiritual empyrean. It is not a mystical union of God and the devotee, locked forever in a pairing of contemplative delight—even though many Christians, including some great theologians and spiritual leaders, have depicted it this way.[14] It is not a return to a primitive state of nature. Nor is it merely a better, safer, more reliable version of what we have here—a so-called happy hunting or fishing ground—although those tribal intuitions, which we see also in Islam's paradise of a fabulous oasis, are closer to the Biblical picture than views that posit a sharp rupture between this world and the next.

What about those visions of heaven in the Book of Revelation? Those heavenly choirs, bizarre beasts, cosmic battles, and such? All but the most literalistic of Biblical interpreters understand most of what John relays in that book to be symbolic. The question is what they are meant to portray, not whether the next life is actually peopled with gigantic horsemen and fierce dragons and huge bowls full of mass destruction.

Christians have disagreed with each other about the mysterious question of "the intermediate state"—the condition of believers between their deaths and the Second Coming of Jesus when all will be raised from the dead: some to judgment and some to everlasting blessing. Do souls separate from bodies at death and, while the latter decay, enjoy the company of other "dearly departed" and of the Lord in heaven, awaiting the Last Day? Maybe. Many Christians think so, according to various hints in the Bible. Others think it makes more sense to consider us "offline" when we die—just stopped dead—only to be restarted at the Last Judgment in a resurrected state. Either way, the "intermediate state" isn't the final state. The final destiny of our race and our world is not something else, somewhere else, but rebirth and maturation: becoming better and better versions of ourselves on the planet created to be our home.

Indeed, these twin themes of continuity and improvement are confirmed in the brief appearances of the one person who did come back from the dead and show us a bit of what it's like on the other side: the Lord Jesus after Easter. We'll discuss death and resurrection later, but for now we need to mine his story for clues about the world to come and what our best life looks like.

The resurrected Jesus clearly is still Jesus. He is recognizable as such by his disciples. In fact, he looks so much like an ordinary man, rather than some glowing, larger-than-life deity, that Mary Magdalene, weeping outside his tomb as she supposes someone has stolen his body, initially mistakes him for the gardener (John 20:1– 15). He appears to other disciples and specifically says that he is not a ghost, but a renewed, fleshly human being:

> "Look at my hands and my feet; see that it is I myself. Touch me and see; for a ghost does not have flesh and bones as you see that I have." And when he had said this, he showed them his hands and his feet. While in their joy they were disbelieving and still wondering, he said to them, "Have you anything here to eat?" They gave him a piece of broiled fish, and he took it and ate in their presence. (Luke 24:39–42)

Presumably the text mentions Jesus's hands and feet because they bore scars that Doubting Thomas wanted to inspect to make sure Jesus was who and what he said he was (John 20). But what about those scars? Will resurrected bodies be marked by the same injuries and debilities our initial bodies suffered?

Presumably not, since some of those injuries or debilities resulted in our deaths, so they can hardly persist in the world to come. Jesus himself doesn't look like his beaten, bloody self on the evening of his crucifixion, but someone so healthy that he is taken for a gardener, not a reanimated corpse. So Jesus's scars are just that—scars, not open wounds—and he bears some of them as badges of honor, perhaps somewhat like the way some soldiers, peace officers, and athletes bear their scars and even modestly show them to intimates. The overarching principle here is that whatever is good in this life passes over into the next—or something better replaces it. Only that which continues to serve a good purpose continues into the world to come, such as Jesus's telltale scars on hands and feet but not every wound he suffered from his torturers.

At the other end of the metaphysical scale, some Christians have concluded from the bits and pieces of Jesus's post-resurrection appearances that our resurrected bodies, like his, will have supernatural powers—to appear and disappear, to pass through locked doors, and to travel distances at will (see Luke 24 and John 20). Yet the Book of Acts records the Holy Spirit whisking an early preacher, Philip, from one place to another without attributing special powers to Philip himself (Acts 8). So we must be careful not to over-interpret what we see in Jesus's case. In fact, the continuities are far more plentiful and striking than the discontinuities in Jesus's resurrection. He seems, indeed, like his old self—just perfectly healthy.

The Biblical picture of the next life is not of an escape from this current form of life into one radically different, but of the rescue of this form of life, and this very planet, into a renewal of optimal function. Shalom is everything good about this world carried over and improved. The world to come is not a brand-new, "out of nothing" creation—for then we ourselves would be lost as denizens of the old world!—but a repaired planet Earth governed by rehabilitated lords (ourselves) such that all creatures thrive and everyone and everything enjoys a proper relationship with each other and with God. This is the end for which God created the world, an end which does not take leave of, but instead completes and then infinitely extends, the story begun at creation.

I want to emphasize this theme of continuity and improvement in three more respects. First, the Christian view of the next life has often been wrongly portrayed, even by Christians, as some sort of radical break with this world. Consequently, many Christians have understood this world to be, at worst, a prison to escape and a foe to be fought, or at best a pile of resources to be exploited and discarded on the way to "a better place." Christianity, properly understood, deeply values this planet as our initial and eternal home, a home to be cherished and shared lovingly with our fellow creatures.

Second, we were created to value both the material and the spiritual, and thus to enjoy the full scope of creaturely life. Christianity does not ignore the physical in order to concentrate on the spiritual, as many religions do, nor does it focus on material security, comfort, and pleasure to the denigration of spiritual life, the way many of us seem to do. In the Christian view of things, everything matters. The whole creation was pronounced "very good" (Genesis 1:31). And our final hope is a healthier, more beautiful, more resilient, more stable, and more dazzling version of this (whole) life, not some particular dimension of this existence carved off and absolutized, whether spiritual or material.

Lest this all sound too gauzily vague, consider motorcycles. If you have ridden one, you know how thrilling it is to do so. Will there be motorcycles in the world to come? Yes, there will—or there will be something better. Perhaps gravity-defying "speeders," such as those in the *Star Wars* movies. Perhaps winged horses, as in the Pegasus myth. Or perhaps our bodies themselves will be capable of flight. Whatever turns out to be the case, *we won't be disappointed*. The best food, the best drink, the best sport, the best art, the best science, the best handcrafts, the best philosophy, and the best comedy—all that is good will roll on, or be translated/transmuted/transposed into something even better.

Third, if this picture of things is true, then everything we do in this life bears more than a passing resemblance to what we will do in the life to come. Skills we develop (or neglect) in this world will carry over in usefulness to the next. Virtues we cultivate (or neglect) in this life will mark us in the life to come. Everything we are and do now, therefore, matters quite a lot, as we are already living the one life we will ever live—interrupted, yes, as it will be by death, but only *interrupted*. We are, today, here, now, on the trajectory that bends over the horizon to whatever destiny is the logical result of our choices. Our lives, therefore, are of great consequence, however little or even pathetic they might seem to us (or to others). Indeed, they are of eternal consequence, since human beings were made to enjoy eternal life.

For the Christian religion there are only two paths, with their respective destinations of eternal moment: life or death, a world full of blessing so splendid that the best of this world only approximates it, or an everlasting separation from all that is good. And, like Adam and Eve and every human being since them, we get to choose which path we will tread.

Why, then, does the world we inhabit only occasionally, partially, and fitfully resemble that world the Bible promises? What happened to bring us to our current state? And how do we get there from here?

What Is Wrong: Sin and Evil

The Bible's initial picture of a blissful original creation takes up all of two chapters. By Genesis 3, there's trouble—trouble that takes most of the rest of the Bible to redress. In fact, the gorgeous portrait of a resplendent New Jerusalem in the age to come doesn't arrive until the last two chapters of Revelation. Between its first two chapters and last two chapters, the Bible focuses on problem and solution. So: to the problem.

The story in Genesis 3 doesn't seem like much. But let's go slowly through it. In fact, a lot happens very quickly in this highly compressed narrative.

To Adam and Eve, the primeval humans of this creation story, God gives the Garden of Eden—and, by extension, the whole world. Every edible plant God welcomes them to eat, a cornucopia on every side. The fruit of just one tree is off limits, a tree with the intriguing designation of "the knowledge of good and evil." Theologians, poets, and painters have mused about this tree, its fruit, and its powers. At the most basic level, however, the tree is simply "that which is forbidden." It could, therefore, be any tree, since the point is believing and obeying God rather than choosing for oneself, not any magic in the plant itself. And disobeying that forbidding by eating the fruit of that tree would bring one thing Adam and Eve don't have so far: knowledge of evil.

They already know good, of course. They live in Eden! And they are themselves moral innocents. All they know, all they have experienced so far, is good. The one kind of knowledge that distrusting and disobeying God will give them is knowledge of evil. And the very act of considering whether to trust and obey God is the beginning of that rupture in their souls: the tiny, lethal division between good and evil, life and death, communion with God and alienation from God.

The story has its subtleties. The talking serpent, later identified in Jewish and Christian lore with the great opponent of God and humanity, Satan (whose very name in Hebrew means "adversary"), here chats with Eve and poses an apparently silly question: "Did God say, 'You shall not eat from any tree in the garden'?" It seems a silly question, of course, because if God had indeed issued such a command, Adam and Eve might have starved.

The woman replies, "We may eat of the fruit of the trees in the garden; but God said, 'You shall not eat of the fruit of the tree that is in the middle of the garden, nor shall you touch it, or you shall die.'" The conversation lurches from one extreme to the other. God didn't forbid them to eat from any tree, as the serpent suggests, and God also did not command them not even to touch the fruit of the forbidden tree. Neither the serpent nor Eve is dealing with what God actually said. They are trading in nonsensical, exaggerated versions of it. Nonsensical options in moral choice are easily dispensed with, and they are here.

The serpent then makes his decisive move: "But the serpent said to the woman, 'You will not die; for God knows that when you eat of it your eyes will be opened, and you will be like God [or a god—the Hebrew can be rendered either way], knowing good and evil.'" Having established a nonsensical conversation about things God did not actually say, the serpent now sweeps all prohibition off the table, bundling in the actual command of God with their silly caricatures of it. (How often do we do the same when confronted by inconvenient moral strictures: reduce them to cartoon versions and then toss them aside as undeserving of serious reflection, let alone obedience?) It's *all* nonsense, the serpent asserts. Worse, God is holding back something important from Eve and Adam: moral autonomy, the freedom and dignity of deciding for themselves—as do the gods.

Well, now, thinks Eve. That's something to consider. "The woman saw that the tree was good for food"—and nourishment is a basic good, right?—"and that it was a delight to the eyes"—and beauty is a basic good also, right?—"and that the tree was to be desired to make one wise"—and surely wisdom is a basic good? The very definition of evil, to flatly disobey a straightforward command of God, is translated here into terms of fundamental goodness. Eve's rationalization takes only a nudge or two from the serpent, and "she took of its fruit and ate; and she also gave some to her husband, who was with her, and he ate."

Just like that. Enough confusion and deception that the initial moral injunction is occluded; the promise of a good to be gained that is unobtainable by obedience (typical of wicked characters in fairy stories: an attractive gift, outside the normal bounds, that promises special powers but brings awful consequences); a rationalization to transmute evil into good; and—there we are.[15]

Not just Adam and Eve: us. There *we* are. We are our parents' children. This is, according to the Christian understanding of things, the Basic Problem. We disrupt shalom. From the seamless web of loving interactions characteristic of Eden, and especially the benefit of being guided by the wise hand of the Supreme Being, we tear ourselves away in a fit of self-determination. We decide that we will be like the gods, like God, deciding for *ourselves*, damn it, about good and evil. Should a particular religion or philosophy meet with our approval, we will adopt it. Should a particular organization or movement advance our agenda, we will support it. Should a particular person please us, we will connect with him or her—until such time as the relationship proves unsatisfying (= evil), at which point we will choose the good (= terminate it).

Augustine, among many other theologians, identified pride, putting oneself at the center of things, as the deadliest sin. In recent years, feminist theologians have suggested that for some people, more commonly women than men, self-abnegation instead is the fundamental problem—giving up one's proper dignity to serve another: a man, a parent, a child, a cause. I submit that even more basic than either of these deadly sins is the decision to determine for oneself what is most important, what is good and what is evil. And if one is choosing for oneself rather than submitting to God, then one is putting something or someone else in the place of God, which the Bible calls *idolatry*. That is the heart of the human problem: the heart.

Not our emotions per se. Not "heart" in the Valentine's Day sense, but in the Hebrew sense of the very core of ourselves, the "heartwood" of our being. The fundamental problem of humanity is not ignorance. It's true, of course, that we don't know all we need to know to live well. But it's also true that we deny or distort even what we do know in order to wrench it into line with our purposes. And that's a moral problem, not an intellectual one.

In fact, it's not even quite a moral problem. It's not that we cannot discern genuine good from real evil. Most of us retain enough of our original, God-given moral sense to agree on a general ethic that is found the world over: don't kill innocents; love your family; don't exploit the weak; show compassion and generosity; don't lie; keep loyal; and so on. The problem is not fundamentally that we don't know the good so much as that we refuse, and often, to perform the good we know we should do. We do whatever we please. *Autonomy* (literally, being a law unto oneself) is the problem.

And why? Genesis says why. Going it alone, we depart from the most fundamental moral power of all: relationship with God. Instead of benefiting from the wisdom and care of the Creator, who presumably could be trusted to give us only good counsel and ethical encouragement, we prefer to be left to our own devices. The history of humanity demonstrates the consequences, as do the histories of our own lives.

Even this early story in Genesis hints at the horrors to come. "Then the eyes of both were opened, and they knew that they were naked; and they sewed fig leaves together and made loincloths for themselves." In one way, the serpent was quite right. In their moral naïveté, Adam and Eve did lack a certain kind of knowledge. And now, having chosen for themselves, they have it. Their eyes are opened and they see—what? "That they were naked." Instead of the exuberant innocence of the laughing toddler dashing away from the amused parent trying to get her into her diaper and clothes, utterly free and delighted toward the world and expecting nothing but affirmation from the world in return, Adam and Eve see themselves as vulnerable, small, awkward, and shameful. They set to work on the pitiable task of gathering the largest leaves around, fig leaves, and then miserably sit down to fumblingly sew them into covering—any covering. Bound together now by their common sin, rather than by shalom, paradoxically they cooperate to create garments of separation from each other, and from the rest of the world. The shattering of creation's initial unity into fragments of alienation shows up here, immediately. The pink and gold life of the nascent creation has already begun to decay as quickly as those leaves.

The alienation is absolute. They try to hide even from God. "They heard the sound of the Lord God walking in the garden at the time of the evening breeze, and the man and his wife hid themselves from the presence of the Lord God among the trees of the garden." As pathetic as were their efforts to shield themselves from each other and the rest of creation through their leafy aprons, trying to hide from the Creator is sadder, crazier, still.

God plays along, however; the story is not without its darkly comic aspects. "But the Lord God called to the man, and said to him, 'Where are you?'" It's not as if the Supreme Being didn't know where Adam was, of course. God gives the man an opportunity to come clean. And he does, but only after a fashion.

"He said, 'I heard the sound of you in the garden, and I was afraid, because I was naked; and I hid myself.'" So far, so good. Adam is responding with straightforward truth. But not for long, alas.

God replies, "Who told you that you were naked? Have you eaten from the tree of which I commanded you not to eat?" Who told you that you were other than you should be? Why do you no longer feel free and innocent? That could mean only one thing: Did you break the one rule I gave you?

The man has a second opportunity to step up and take responsibility. Seeing a possible escape route, however, the man does what so many of us do. He points at someone else. "The woman whom you gave to be with me, she gave me fruit from the tree, and I ate." He points with one hand at the woman and with the other at God. "*You,*" he says to the Almighty, "gave her to me, and *she* gave me the fruit. All I did was eat. So let's bear in mind the mitigating circumstances of your giving me this woman who then put temptation in my way."

God decides not to reply right away to this early exercise in buck-passing and instead addresses the woman: "What is this that you have done?"

The woman, who has now learned something about her husband she didn't know before—what knowledge she is gaining!— also learns something *from* him and likewise engages in dodging blame: "The serpent tricked me, and I ate."

Any parent would be deeply disappointed in such answers from his or her children. How sad God must have been—as God surely is at my own paltry attempts at excuse and offloading of my guilt on others. God turns to the serpent.

The serpent is apparently someone with whom God is already well acquainted, since God doesn't bother interrogating the beast. Instead, God levels judgment:

> "Because you have done this,
>> cursed are you among all animals
>> and among all wild creatures;
> upon your belly you shall go,
>> and dust you shall eat
>> all the days of your life.
> I will put enmity between you and the woman,
>> and between your offspring and hers;
> he will strike your head,
>> and you will strike his heel."

The serpent will crawl along the earth, the lowest of the low, with dust perpetually in its face. And this nice little relationship newly hatched between the serpent and the woman? It's over. Forever. In fact, you and her offspring will engage in mutual harm: as he comes down crushingly on your head, you'll rise up one last time to bite his heel.

Then God turns to the woman and tells her that her distinctive task and position in the original creation mandate God gave to humanity—to procreate together, man and woman, in order to co-create together, man and woman—will now be much worse than they would have been.

> "To the woman he said,
> 'I will greatly increase your pangs in childbearing;
>> in pain you shall bring forth children,
> yet your desire shall be for your husband,
>> and he shall rule over you.'"

Procreation will now be an ordeal. And the original partnership with her husband will also be an ordeal. She will be inescapably drawn to him even as he rules over her, rather than the two of them having dominion over the rest of creation as a single cooperative unit, together.

God finally turns to the man and says that the cultivation of the earth, the other part of the "procreate to co-create" commandment, will also be made more difficult:

> "Because you have listened to the voice of your wife,
>   and have eaten of the tree
> about which I commanded you,
>   'You shall not eat of it,'
> cursed is the ground because of you;
>   in toil you shall eat of it all the days of your life;
> thorns and thistles it shall bring forth for you;
>   and you shall eat the plants of the field.
> By the sweat of your face
>   you shall eat bread
> until you return to the ground,
>   for out of it you were taken;
> you are dust,
>   and to dust you shall return."

So much for being "like gods." Adam, you'll have to work the ground hard just to stay alive. And you won't stay alive forever, but instead, very unlike a god, you'll return to the dust from which you were made.

God then confirms the new situation in graphic fashion: "the Lord God made garments of skins for the man and for his wife, and clothed them."[16] But there is one more important thing to do:

> Then the Lord God said, "See, the man has become like one of
> us, knowing good and evil; and now, he might reach out his hand

and take also from the tree of life, and eat, and live forever"—
therefore the Lord God sent him forth from the garden of Eden,
to till the ground from which he was taken. He drove out the man;
and at the east of the garden of Eden he placed the cherubim, and
a sword flaming and turning to guard the way to the tree of life.

We are told nothing about this second mysterious tree. What
is clear is that paradise is lost. Life as we have known it ever
since—hard, dangerous, and limited—begins. Immortality has
vanished, yes, but also shalom now seems very far away. For the
corrupting stain of sin—the choosing for oneself, with all its baleful
consequences—is now a family attribute. The very next story in the
Bible is that of Cain and Abel, sons of Adam and Eve, two brothers
who initially do the right thing—bring a ritual sacrifice to God—
and then end up terribly wrong.

You likely know the story, recorded in Genesis 4:

Now Abel was a keeper of sheep, and Cain a tiller of the
ground. In the course of time Cain brought to the Lord an offering of the fruit of the ground, and Abel for his part brought
of the firstlings of his flock, their fat portions. And the Lord
had regard for Abel and his offering, but for Cain and his offering he had no regard. So Cain was very angry, and his countenance fell. The Lord said to Cain, "Why are you angry, and
why has your countenance fallen? If you do well, will you not
be accepted?"

The story doesn't tell us what was deficient about Cain's offering.
Interestingly, however, Cain doesn't ask what was deficient. Cain
doesn't seek clarity from God about what it would mean to "do
well" and then follow it to make things right. Instead, just like Mom
and Dad did, Cain chooses to decide about good and evil for himself and takes matters into his own hands. "Cain said to his brother
Abel, 'Let us go out to the field.' And when they were in the field,

Cain rose up against his brother Abel, and killed him." There, now. Sorted.

But no. God shows up again. (However absent God seems to be, God always eventually shows up, and God always knows what's been going on.) As God did with Cain's father, God asks Cain to account for himself. "Where is your brother Abel?"

Cain infamously replies, "I do not know; am I my brother's keeper?"

Well, perhaps not. But you are your brother's murderer, Cain, the very opposite of your brother's keeper (that is, protector, preserver from harm, as the *keep* in a castle where one hides one's treasures and one's family from attack). You are the very opposite of the big brother looking out for the younger one. Thus the pattern established by the (first) parents is repeated, with God holding the human responsible for what he has done, setting out the awful entailments with more curses on the very nature of human life, the cultivation of the earth:

And the Lord said, "What have you done? Listen; your brother's blood is crying out to me from the ground! And now you are cursed from the ground, which has opened its mouth to receive your brother's blood from your hand. When you till the ground, it will no longer yield to you its strength; you will be a fugitive and a wanderer on the earth.

Adam and Eve poison themselves and the garden. Cain now poisons the earth. How quickly the story has moved, from the Garden of Eden and the prospect of worldwide shalom to—this: the layering on of sin—individual, familial, corporate, national—until we arrive at today's global dysfunction, alienation, guilt, and pain. This is the phenomenon of *sin*, not just "sins." Yes, we have each done many bad things and failed to do many good things. That's bad enough. But we sin because we are sin-full. We are, I'm sorry to say, rotten to the core. We sin sometimes because we *like* sinning. We *prefer* to do wrong. Wickedness, as so many advertisers know, *tastes good* to us. And that's true for individuals and for groups, even whole societies. What begins as choice becomes, in the individual, habit and, eventually, disposition. What begins as choice becomes, in the group, custom and, eventually, tradition. In individuals and groups, even the whole human race, what begins in Eden as *choice* very quickly becomes *trait*, a condition of our hearts.

Humanity's earliest generations, according to these ancient tales in Genesis, utterly failed in their calling. And we have kept the family traditions alive, haven't we, each in our own way?

We look around and see vestiges of Eden everywhere, in the gorgeous landscapes of our planet and the shimmering glory of a snowflake. We look around and rejoice in the triumphs of human cultivation: splendid apples, glorious cathedrals, ingenious cell phones, dazzling scientific theories, moving symphonies, and yes, magnificent gardens. But also: vandalism and waste and absurdity, greed and deceit and scandal, abuse and exploitation and cruelty, stupidity and stubbornness and envy. Petty slights and state-sponsored horrors. Needless irritation and regime-wide oppression. Awful. And it's everywhere, affecting everyone and everything.

It is so very far from here back to Eden, or forward to the New Jerusalem. What can possibly be done?

The Christian replies: what has been done, what is being done, and what will be done. Let's find out what that means.

What Can Be Done: Initial Options

What needs to be done? Since it seems that we human beings caused the problem, one would fairly conclude that the solution should come from us, too. But since we ourselves *are* the problem, how can we also be the solution? Don't we need help from outside ourselves even to do what we ought to do to repair the damage and set things right?[17]

Christianity says yes to both questions.

What needs to be done is in fact unfathomably complex. But perhaps a simple figure can help us grasp the essentials. Think of a vertical line with a horizontal "zero line" bisecting it halfway up. The lower end of the line symbolizes our negative state as sinners: people who have sinned and who are disposed to keep sinning. These two negatives need removal and remediation. First, we need our sins forgiven. Second, we need our inclination toward evil, our appetite for evil—the hunger for it, the pleasure we take in it—excised. We need our lusts and resentments and hatreds quenched.

If these two negatives could be addressed somehow, that would bring us up to the zero line. If we stopped here, things would be much better than they were, of course. We wouldn't have an evil record anymore for which we deserve to be punished, nor would we be afflicted with inclinations toward evil that keep pulling us into trouble. But there would be no positives there. We would be merely "not negative."

So here we need a fresh start, what the Bible sometimes calls a "new birth" and theologians call "regeneration." The old is gone; the new stretches ahead. Every fairy tale and every story of redemption features this scene, this liminal place in which the protagonist finally, decisively, can break from his past. He has made the clean break. But now he needs a new beginning, a new identity, a new direction, if he isn't going to be dogged and dragged down continually by his past. Jesus understood this reality and flatly told one inquirer, who wanted merely to become a better person than he currently was, "You must be born again" (John 3:1–7). Improvement won't do. Dying to the old life and starting a new one: that's what's required.

Now, it's not like we stop being anything like who we were. We don't become completely different people. Instead, all that was good about us before needs to be freed from all that was bad; whatever good we lacked needs to be given to us; and the good now within us—actual or merely potential—gets an opportunity to grow into maturity. We need renewal, not just progress.

If we stopped at this stage, at the "zero line," we'd be only spiritual infants, like Adam and Eve were. We would be freshly innocent, yes, but we would also be wide open to a new round of temptation and failure. We need to keep ascending the line toward maturity, toward the realization of our potential: seeds growing into trees and babies growing into adults. Theologians call this process "sanctification," the process of becoming holy (from the Latin *sanctus*). Moral soundness is part of that concept, but its fundamental idea is of being *sacred*, of being "set apart for special use" by God. As we grow up, we become more and more dedicated to God: more and more useful to God as we connect with God more fully and frequently, as we become less confused and more clear-minded, as we become less distracted and more dedicated, as we become less stupid and more skilled, as we become less greedy and more giving.

There is no reason to suppose that this upward trend has a terminus. In the world to come, we won't become suddenly omniscient, and there is no reason to think we will become spiritually or aesthetically perfect, either. There will always be more to learn, to experience, to enjoy. But we will have shed our ancient inclination to stray from God. The fissure in our hearts will have closed. We just won't find sin interesting anymore. We will instead have a constant, confirmed attachment to God and all that is good, placing every one of our steps rightly on the path of life, rather than wandering, sauntering, or hurrying off of it, as we currently are inclined every day to do.

This confirmation of character, this moral goodness we can attain and enjoy, is what keeps the whole thing from reverting back to another Eden and yet another Fall. (Students always ask me about that: "If we get a new start, what's to prevent the whole sad round from starting again?") The difference is that now, through sanctification, our desires are reoriented. The cheap candy we found delightful as children we now judge to be unpalatably sickly sweet.

The fast food we couldn't chomp down fast enough as teenagers revolts us in our middle age. What seemed glamorous when we were young seems merely vulgar from a mature perspective.

In moral terms, we will have no desire to sin, just as a loving mother has no desire to torture her children, just as a patriot has no desire to betray his country. In fact, "lack of desire" is far from the right way to put it. The very idea of sin, of defying our gracious God and militating against shalom, will be at once both obviously insane and immediately horrific. That's what moral maturity looks like, and that's what we all can eventually enjoy.

So between that splendid state of virtue and our current one, a lot has to happen—to each of us as individuals, and to society as a whole. We will need divine assistance to accomplish all that needs doing, since human history shows our race's conspicuous inability to make ourselves or our civilizations even close to what we ought to be. So what has God done, what is God doing, and what will God do?

The long answer is a long answer indeed: the entire Bible, and the chain of events it describes from the very beginning of human history. All of that is rather more than I'm prepared to take on at the moment. There is, conveniently, a short answer. It is the one every kid in Sunday school knows: *Jesus.* To understand the short answer properly, however, requires us to understand at least something of the long answer. So let's see if we can get Jesus into focus with a short sketch of his Biblical context.

The first thing to say is that the long answer is a very long answer. If you or I were to try to fix what's wrong with the world, and we had the resources of a Supreme Being, we would probably act like gods do in other religions. We would communicate The Truth in ways people could accept and understand. We would speak through sacred teachers, holy role models, and inspired mass media (scriptures, for instance), with all of them validated in ways appropriate to the message and the messengers: signs and wonders indicating supernatural authority. In tribal situations we would appoint charismatic leaders to inform, transform, and reform the tribe as necessary, while great missionary religions would be commissioned to spread The Truth across cultural lines and set up exemplary communities of the converted.

All of this has, in fact, happened, and with much evident good result. All over the world the religions that have come to dominate are, for all the manifest faults in their followers and in some of their less laudable varieties, so much better than what they replaced. None of them, for instance, practices human sacrifice, or even much in the way of animal sacrifice. The divine is less to be feared and placated than honored and obeyed. Most of the world's religions insist on the kindly care of children, many teach compassion for the weak and needy, and all of them demand adherence to a moral code that includes the virtues of honesty, loyalty, industriousness, cooperation, self-respect, self-control, justice, and more. In general—and, again, acknowledging ugly exceptions around the globe—today's religions have improved the world.

If these religions were all that was required to right what is wrong with the world, however, wouldn't the world be righted by now, given that one or another of these major religions has dominated the world's leading civilizations for a millennium or more? Yet something still seems to be quite wrong. Even the noblest of these religions have been co-opted and enlisted in aid of quests for the perennial desiderata of territory, wealth, and prestige. We humans seem to take whatever good we're given, including religious insight, and shape it according to our will to power. Education and training, no matter how extensive, seem insufficient to make us good. We need, it seems, to be saved from ourselves.

The God of the Bible is willing to undertake that project, and God takes an astonishingly long view of it. God starts the plan of salvation in the ancient world in an unlikely place in an unlikely way. Instead of originating the One True Way with a particular religious genius—a Laozi or a Buddha or a Zoroaster—he selects what, by the sacred account itself, is a pretty ordinary man and promises that, if this man will trust and obey God, God will make of this man a great nation. Moreover, this eventual nation will provide the salvation of the world—but way, way down the road.[18]

So this man, Abram (later called Abraham), in ancient Mesopotamia, leaves the comfort and security of urban life and travels a very long way—almost from one end of the Fertile Crescent to the other. He arrives in what seems unpromising country indeed, what we now know as Israel. And for the rest of his life, this city man lives in tents as a pastoralist.

He has a couple of sons—and they both become fathers of nations: Ishmael, ancestor of Arabs, and Isaac, ancestor of Jews. Through the latter line comes Abraham's grandson Jacob, later known as Israel, and, following the move of Jacob and his family to Egypt for respite during a famine, four centuries later his descendants have become numerous enough to worry the pharaoh. This pharaoh decides to enslave the Israelites to keep this potential fifth column within his borders weak and docile. Enter Moses, whom God appoints the leader of his people to rescue them in the Exodus (Greek for "exit"), the event that marks Israel as a coherent nation as they move as one into the desert on their way to the Promised Land—that unpromising land once inhabited by their patriarch, Abraham.

Along the way, at Mount Sinai, God gives Moses a set of laws to guide the life of God's special people. The Ten Commandments are the most famous part of this *torah* (= "law, instruction"), but it includes much else—for God is interested in all of life, not just certain religious or moral aspects of it. God is the God of shalom, and Torah was given to teach Israel, and through the example of Israel the rest of the world, a sense of how a properly governed nation should live.[19]

At the heart of the community life specified in Torah was the nation's relationship to God, mediated through a class of priests and a set of rituals. These symbolically fraught persons and practices spoke of God's *transcendence*. Increasingly Israel would realize that their God wasn't just *their* God, but the one true God, the God above all. This worship of God also signified God's *immanence*, God's willingness to live with people and participate in their affairs. It pictured the dreadful and daily reality of human sin, as each morning and afternoon priests would offer expiatory sacrifices for the transgressions of the people. And it assured Israel that God loved them, wanted the best for them, and would do all God could to help them—including forgiving those sins and teaching them a better way.

This arrangement, however, might have been all very well for a tiny Levantine nation, but what about the rest of the world? And that ancient code, however impressive it might seem in comparison with the alternatives on offer in the ancient Near East (and it is impressive, especially in its relatively benign treatment of women, children, and foreigners), can hardly guide us in the vastly more complex world of modernity.[20] So how does all that, back there and then, have any real implication for us here and now?

Furthermore, if we think about those Israelite temple rituals, how is it that sacrifices of plants and animals, no matter how symbolically rich and humbly offered, can actually do anything to atone for the crimes of human beings? Other cultures came to the conclusion that only *human* sacrifice can make right what human transgression has made wrong. Why doesn't Israel come to that conclusion? And, since none of us are advocating human sacrifice today, what then can *we* do to make right what we have made wrong?

What Can Be Done: Religious Options

Before we continue our look at Christianity's distinctive teaching, a little context from religious studies in general can help us. The world's religions are vast and complex. But each features one or more of the following four dynamics in the interaction of human beings with the rest of the world, and especially with whatever higher powers there may be. We can range them across a spectrum of human action, from an exclusive focus upon individual responsibility to the prospect of a relationship with a helpful deity: magic, moralism, mysticism, and salvation.

Magic is at one end of this range. I don't mean magic in the sense of supernatural powers possessed by extraordinary individuals, but magic as something anyone can do, once you've been taught the spell. Magic of this sort is essentially transactional, even mechanical. That's why it is often understood as a progenitor of, or in some respects a rival to, science and technology. Magic is manipulation. Do the correct thing with the correct materials in the correct way at the correct time in the correct place and—*voilà!* One gets what one wants. Magic is a vending machine. Provide the right inputs, get the right outputs. Whatever spookiness might attend it is rather beside the point, no more odd in its way than the oddities of scientists and engineers with their peculiar jargon, clothing, equipment, laboratories, and activities. Magic is the approach that sees the universe as amenable to power properly deployed. Learn the proper deployments, use them, and the universe cooperates. It's up to you. And plenty of religion is like this, of course, from praying certain formulaic prayers to offering to the gods certain approved substances on auspicious dates in sacred spaces. Do this, get that.

Moralism is also entirely up to us. Moralism is the form of religion that understands the universe, or at least the Ultimate Power that governs the universe, as possessing an ethical code. Learn that code and fulfill it, and you will achieve whatever ultimate good is to be had. Moralism defines Confucianism, for instance. Behave yourself properly, in public and private, according to the traditions of Confucian philosophy, and you and all those who similarly behave will reap the supreme benefit for which Confucianism was devised: social harmony. "We shall have proper government when the prince is [or 'behaves properly as'] a prince, the master is a master, the father is a father, and the son is a son" (*Analects*, XII.11). Moralism also is the root of the Indian karma-dharma complex. Each morally significant action (karma) is either good or bad according to the ethical structure of the cosmos as pertinent to one's particular status in this lifetime. Behave properly (according to one's duty, or dharma), and one will be reincarnated on a higher level as a matter of course. It's not unlike gravity. Behave badly and descend—again, ipso facto. Buddhism advises one to follow the Noble Eightfold Path to everlasting bliss (nirvana as understood by most Buddhists today)—or, as we have seen, at least the extinguishing of desire and suffering (the Theravadin understanding of nirvana). Daoism, Epicureanism, Stoicism, and all similar philosophies agree that our well-being depends for the most part on acknowledging, and conforming our ways to, the way of the world. (Those who look nowadays to evolutionary biology for moral norms practice a religion of this sort, even as, again, they would likely refuse the label "religious.") And even in religions ostensibly centered on devotion to a deity, such as Judaism or Christianity or Islam or *bhakti* Hinduism, a significant degree of moralism obtains. Proper behavior is expected, no matter how gracious God may be. In some popular versions of these faiths, moreover, moralism can sometimes predominate, so that the onus is entirely on oneself and the Deity is reduced to a cosmic judge who simply weighs up one's good and bad deeds and pronounces upon one's life an infallible verdict.

Mysticism moves us into a zone that runs the gamut from heroic ascetic effort to achieve a spiritual oneness with impersonal ultimate reality—as in merging with Brahman, the supreme principle of the universe, as taught in the Advaita Vedanta traditions of Hinduism—to casting oneself joyfully into the love of a personal God, to be engaged in passionate mutual contemplation forever. This latter form of mysticism, the personal form of spiritual union, shows up in various forms of monotheism, including the Abrahamic religions (Judaism, Christianity, and Islam), and also in polytheistic settings in which one fastens on one particular deity as the central, or even exclusive, object of one's love, as in devotional

Hinduism. Mysticism is intensely individualistic, but one is striving to connect with the One who is not merely oneself. One strives to focus upon God, and thus to leave aside everything else, at last to enjoy eternal communion with God—whether in the company of other equally God-focused devotees or not.

Normally, mysticism requires instruction from adepts according to texts and traditions that have been found helpful by those further along the path. How much God assists one in achieving mystical union varies—perhaps very little (in the case of mysticisms involving union with the impersonal, it is hard to see how Brahman, or the like, can be seen as an agent at all) and perhaps quite a lot (as in the ecstasy of one surprisedly ravished by God's attention).

Salvation, however, tilts the balance of responsibility decidedly onto the "God" side of the relationship. In some religious vocabularies, to be sure, "salvation" can mean merely "the accomplishment of escape"—as in *moksha*, in some Indian religions: the escape from the endless cycle of reincarnation, *samsara*, to a happier state "off the wheel." But typically "salvation" means being saved from a bad condition by someone or something else. God assists one to achieve or receive the good that one otherwise would not experience.

Salvation itself is offered in a variety of modes—ranging along a similar spectrum from "some human work required" to "only human acceptance is needed." *Revelation* is God showing us the way things fundamentally are and what needs to be done to make things right, with the implication that if God did not so graciously show us, this crucial truth would remain a mystery. But that wouldn't be *salvation* in the strong sense we're using it here, however, since one would be left to magic, moralism, or mysticism to proceed to the desired end.

Rehabilitation is better, as the deity gets involved such that one's faults are remedied and positive qualities maximized in order that one can now do whatever needs doing. God in this mode provides revelatory instruction and encouragement, yes, but also occasions for gaining insight and practicing virtue, as might be given by a psychological or physical therapist to one who undertakes the regimen he or she prescribes.

Supplementation is more helpful still, with the deity adding resources to help on one's quest. Divine beings might add to a person's stock of talents and abilities such that she is now capable of greater wisdom and goodness, as some kinds of Buddhists pray to buddhas and bodhisattvas for enlightenment. The Helper might do more, actually altering her situation. In Pure Land Buddhism, for example, the generous Amida Buddha brings devotees to his lovely realm, which is entirely conducive to meditation. Thus the achievement of the ultimate goal, nirvana, is made far easier—although one still must achieve it oneself.

Renewal is radical—the provision of a new heart or mind, a fresh start along the path of life. It might come as *satori*, Japanese Buddhism's term for seeing the true nature of things and consequently living on a new plane of awareness. It might come as a mystical vision. It might take the much deeper form of personal rebirth, often signified with a new name—whether via a successful vision quest, as in forms of North American tribal religions, or via the baptism of the Holy Spirit in Christianity.

Each salvation-oriented religion offers one or more of these modalities to provide for the faithful what they cannot provide for themselves. The last mode, *substitution*, is the most radical form of salvation. In this case, God rescues us by doing all the main work necessary. Hinduism sometimes speaks of the "monkey mode" versus the "cat mode" of salvation: in the former, the mother monkey puts down her arm to let the baby crawl up onto her back, and then she carries the baby where they want to go, while in the latter, the mother cat simply bites down gently on her kitten at the scruff of the neck and carries the precious bundle to safety.

Now, then, to the Christian view of things.

What Can Be Done: The Christian View

Four metaphors dominate the Bible's depiction of God's relationship with God's people—that is, those of us who become realigned and reconnected with God. These metaphors combine several dimensions of religion and several modes of salvation.

The first metaphor is that of *patron and client*. Early in the Biblical story, God communicates with Abraham and establishes a covenant with him, an agreement in which each side has obligations to the other. The covenant is not symmetrical. One party is clearly dominant: setting the terms, yes, but also responsible for most of the work that will be done and most of the blessing that will be given. God is the Lord, the sovereign, the One with the power, and Abraham is the one whom the Almighty has chosen to favor. God asks Abraham to cooperate with him in initiating a (very) long-term scheme to bless all the peoples of the world (God doesn't specify how) through Abraham's offspring. Moreover, if Abraham will behave properly—which centrally means to trust God's promises and obey God's commands—then he himself will be blessed. Abraham does his part—albeit stumblingly. (The Hebrew Bible is surprisingly candid about Abraham's serious falterings along the way to becoming an exemplary patriarch.) And God does God's.

In this relationship, we see moralism (correct behavior) and mysticism (encounter with God) and elements of salvation. God provides Abraham with offspring, and riches, and protection from enemies, as well as pardon for Abraham's offenses, some of them serious. At the heart of the relationship, however, is love: not mere sentiment or even strong affection, but deep and active concern for the other's well-being: faithfulness, loyalty, generosity, respect. This is the dominant motif governing the relationship between God and the eventual nation of Israel as well. "I am Yhwh your God who brought you out of the land of Egypt, out of the house of slavery" (Exodus 20:2)—and so God gifts Israel with the wisdom of the Ten Commandments and, indeed, the whole Torah. In doing so, God says, Since I have done this for you, as I promised I would according to the covenant I established with your ancestor Abraham, and since I will continue to hold up my side of the agreement, here is what being faithful to your side of the covenant looks like. You will be my faithful client, and I will be your generous patron.

The second motif is much more intimate, that of *husband and wife*. Given the patriarchal structure of human societies around the world, God takes the role of husband to his people's collective role as wife. God thereby incurs the much larger responsibility to care for God's much less powerful spouse. God furthermore is depicted as courting Israel, marrying Israel, putting up with Israel's religious adultery as Israel worships other gods, even disciplining Israel (an idea that properly startles egalitarian moderns but would make sense in other cultures)—all in order to establish and maintain an eternal relationship of kindness, trust, mutual respect, and fruitfulness.[21]

Here again we see moral expectations. A wife cannot rightly act as if she were single, but instead should act according to the obligations of a healthy marriage. Israel is required to behave faithfully to God. We also see mystical dimensions in the mutual enjoyment of each other in spiritual encounter—although these elements aren't foregrounded in the Old Testament. We certainly see elements of salvation: God rescues Israel from Egypt (in the Exodus), educates Israel (in the Law), gives Israel a home (in the Promised Land), causes Israel to flourish (under Kings Saul, David, and Solomon), forgives Israel's constant failures (in the sacrificial system at the Temple), and even restores Israel after her spiritual adultery (in the Exile to Babylon and Return to the Land).

In the New Covenant (= "New Testament") established by Jesus, these themes are continued. After all, Jesus is Jewish, as are his first followers, and his public career is that of a rabbi, a spiritual teacher. The distinctly Christian understanding of God's relationship with God's people—which will, as the early church spreads, take in the whole world, not just Israel—will presume, not abandon, the earlier models of patron/client and husband/wife. Jesus will be pictured as the fiancé of the Church, and he will be addressed as "Lord" in a way reminiscent of Israel's deference to and dependence upon Yhwh.

Jesus expands the repertoire of motifs, however. He is, indeed, a *rabbi* who gathers a group of followers known as *disciples*—those whom he will discipline, or school, or train. We use "disciple" nowadays to indicate a very strong attachment of pupil to teacher: a concern by the student not merely to be educated by, but to emulate the person of, the master. Jesus also introduces to his followers the idea that they can, and should, properly think of Yhwh as their *Father* and of themselves as God's adopted *children*. He even instructs them to address God as such, as the Lord's Prayer begins, "Our Father, who art in heaven." To be sure, Jesus is, in good rabbinical style, not inventing so much as innovating upon themes already visible in the Hebrew Bible. Those scriptures do depict God as teaching Israel, of course, and even as caring for Israel in parental terms—both maternal and paternal terms, incidentally. But Jesus's innovation is significant. No one in his time would have directly addressed God in such familiar, familial terms as "Father."

These relationships continue the combinations we have seen: moralism (certain behavior is intrinsic to the roles of disciple and child), mysticism (personal communion is a feature of both relationships), and salvation (the master blesses the discipline with life-giving wisdom; the parent gives the child the very gift of life, and so much more besides). Taken together, these four relationships overlap in a rich tableau: patron/client, husband/wife, master/disciple, and parent/child.

So far, so good. The Supreme Being is marvelously benevolent toward God's creatures, and they respond gratefully. But what about sin? And why does Jesus end up on a cross?

The near absence of these two elements—sin and the crucifixion of Jesus—from much of contemporary Christianity has been widely noticed. In our culture generally, sin is frequently euphemized as a lapse of reason ("mistake"), wisdom ("poor judgment"), or etiquette ("indiscretion"). Sometimes it's even dressed up as an excess of virtue: loyalty (to "my family," "my company," "my nation"), ambition (I wanted X "too much" and went after it "too hard"), or passion (I "couldn't help it"). Increasingly, sin is medicalized such that someone caught in a flagrant transgression retreats from the spotlight "to go into treatment." Sin as what it actually is—whether a failure to resist temptation at best, an indulgence in evil desires as usual, or a willful rebellion against moral norms at worst—surfaces only, we like to think, in particularly wicked persons who by definition are abnormal (= not like us).

Indeed, many of us seem to view humanity as divisible into three discrete cohorts. At one end is the small cluster of saints—the Mother Teresas, Mister Rogerses, and other ethical heroes whose lives are incomprehensibly far removed from our own. At the other end are the villains—the Hitlers, Stalins, Maos, and other unfathomably awful people who seem barely human in their appetite for evil. The rest of us are in the middle. Nobody's perfect, of course, but we haven't killed anyone, we're kind to furry animals and children, and we're generally decent folk. Sure, we might curse a bit, and cut a few corners on our taxes, and gossip a little, and flirt once in a while, but hey, that's normal, right?

The Bible, however, says there are only two kinds of people: sinners who are off the path of righteousness and therefore on their way to a lost eternity, and sinners who have been saved by God and returned to the path of righteousness and therefore on their way to a fabulous future. The Bible does not say, as some Christians do, that everyone is simply and entirely terrible. God created humanity in God's own image to make shalom in the world, and to some extent we bear that image and obey that mandate still. Christians should, and many of us do, recognize that our fellow humans are capable of good, even great good, whether or not they are reconciled to God or even believe that God exists. The Bible says, however, that we are all infected by a lethal ethical disease. We are all inclined away from submission to God and toward self-centeredness and autonomy. We are all cursed with a moral appetite that finds at least certain sins attractive, even delicious. We may feel fine, even wholesome, but there is a rot within us that alters the very patterns by which we live day to day. And every once in a while, especially under stress, that malignancy erupts to startle those around us and even shock ourselves.

Thus we reckon with sin. As for crucifixions, we moderns see none except in horrifying movies. We also see nothing like them in the other major world religions. No major religious figure dies a horrible death: not Krishna, not Buddha, not Laozi or Kongzi or Zoroaster, not Moses, and not Muhammad. No major religious figure dies a *redemptive* or *salvific* death as does Jesus, for no other world religion thinks such a drastic act is necessary. If one follows the sage's wisdom, or observes the proper rituals, or adopts the correct forms of life, or worships the right deity, or meditates to the ideal state, or joins in the life of the observant community, then all will be well. In the normal course of things—allowing for extreme situations in which one must defend the righteous community with force—no one and nothing needs to suffer, let alone die.

Except in tribal religions. And Christianity.

Christians throughout the world annually commemorate a horrible event: the crucifixion of a whipped-bloody Jesus on Good Friday. They symbolically eat Christ's body and drink his blood each time they receive Communion—which for many pious Christians is *every day*, and for the majority at least monthly. Human sacrifice? Ritual cannibalism? What in God's name is going on?

Rooms full of books have been written about this subject. But for now, in this small space, let's focus on one distressing detail as a key to the rest. Let's ask a simple, if unsettling, question: What's with all this blood?

Christian blood symbolism harks back to the giving of Torah to Moses by God on Mount Sinai. The heart of all of this legislation and instruction was the sacrificial system maintained by the priests: the round of daily and annual sacrifices in which animals were killed and offered to God on burning altars as substitutes for the human sinners who gave them up. Suffering to make up for sin, and ultimately "life for life," is the basic logic of *atonement*, of making up for whatever wrong has been done. And the spilling of blood is the most powerful of sign of life sacrifice.

The Hebrew prophets made clear that these rituals collectively formed an elaborate picture of God's holiness and our sin. God recognizes sin to be mortally serious. Sin damages and ultimately destroys. Therefore the most graphic symbolism of life and death was necessary to portray both the cost of sin and the price of its redemption. This is a view shared in many other cultures—hence blood sacrifice, including human sacrifice, has been practiced around the globe.

What is striking about the Israelite sacrificial system is not only its tribute to God's holiness, God's loathing of evil and insistence upon its purging, but also the sacrificial system's testimony to God's mercy. God was willing to accept animal substitutes and explicitly forbade human sacrifice, although it makes no apparent sense to draw the line there. How can the blood of bulls or sheep or goats possibly make up for human sin? (One of the later books of prophecy in the Hebrew Bible, in fact, asks questions along these lines: see Micah 6:6–7). Something crucial is missing. The system is radically incomplete, and therefore incompetent. Atonement is not being fully made.

Christian belief recognizes this point and affirms the startling truth that human sacrifice is necessary after all (Hebrews 10:1–18). Only human beings can pay human moral debts, and those debts amount to a weight sufficient to crush the life out of us. Jesus called himself the "Son of Man," an ancient phrase that in his distinctive usage seems to have meant "the representative of humanity," and (in a way no one understands) Jesus took on himself the consequences of all humanity's sin. As the one fully innocent human being who did not deserve to suffer and die coupled with the strength of a god—this combination of human and divine natures is essential to understanding how Jesus did what he did—Jesus underwent the suffering and death due to each and all of us as our scapegoat, as "the Lamb of God who takes away the sins of the world" (John 1:29). Somehow Jesus was able to substitute for the rest of us. The blood symbolism of Jesus's Cross therefore makes sense, albeit very grim sense: suffering for sin and life for life. In this Great Exchange, as Martin Luther puts it, Christ receives the consequences of our sin while we receive the benefits of his goodness.

Understandably, many people have been appalled at this whole idea. They have seen in this scenario a hapless victim of a deity's bloodthirsty rage. How could God do that to Jesus? Here we must invoke what can seem to be a highly abstruse idea—the doctrine of the Trinity. Orthodox Christianity believes in one God who somehow exists as three Persons: Father, Son, and Holy Spirit. Christians do not understand *how* this one God can somehow exist in three persons, and we have no really good analogy to help us understand this assertion.[22] What we do have, however, is evidence that God exists this way. And, just as in science, when we have evidence for things we do not (yet) understand, we nonetheless believe in them. Christianity has concluded that the best way to construe all the data we have about God and Jesus and the Holy Spirit—in Scripture and in the experience of Christians—is to view the Three as also One, as Trinity.

Since this point matters a very great deal, we need to pause here for a few more minutes before we can understand the figure on the Cross. Christianity emerges out of Israel's religion, what by Jesus's day was known as Judaism. "Jesus himself was a Jew, as were almost all of his first followers. The one thing Jews were known for in the Roman Empire was their steadfast adherence to monotheism: one and only one God. The Romans, with a plenitude of gods for every occasion and locale (as was typical of most ancient societies), looked askance at the Jews for their narrow-mindedness, even as they admired the antiquity and perseverance of Jewish beliefs. The point for us is that no people in the world were less inclined to believe in the plurality of the divine nature than the Jews.

Jesus's disciples, however, very early came to believe they ought to worship him—not just to venerate him as their esteemed rabbi, but to give him the honor due to God, including praying to him.[23] How the early Christian experience of Jesus led the disciples to worship him and then conceptually wrestle with the idea of a "two-part" God is a long and interesting story. This process soon eventuates in belief in a "three-part" God, as the Holy Spirit, previously understood as just another name for the influence of Yhwh in the world, comes into focus as a distinct Person, capable of loving and powerful agency and One on whom the early Christians came to rely as their constant companion once Jesus had left the earth after his resurrection (John 14:16–17).

We are racing ahead of the narrative, of course. The main point here is simply that Jesus so impressed his followers with his God-like wisdom, compassion, and power that they were compelled to revise their understanding of God in a truly innovative, if also deeply mysterious, way—at first a "binitarian" view of God, and then fairly quickly a *trinitarian* view of God. Their experience of the Holy Spirit, coupled with the way Jesus spoke about the Spirit (particularly in John 13–17), led them to this three-in-one conviction.

Who could come up with something like the doctrine of the Trinity unless circumstances compelled them to do so? The oddity of this belief does not, of course, imply anything about its truth. But as we return now to Jesus on the Cross, this strange, if not simply incoherent, idea will do some important conceptual work for us.

If we take the Christian view of Trinity, the Cross of Christ is not properly understood as a big Father-God angrily pounding a small Son-God to death. Instead, the Cross-event features the suffering of One God—one deity suffering as Father, Son, and Spirit: as the Victim on the Cross, yes, but also as the loving Father and Spirit who hate to see him hurt, even as they support him in his necessary work. So there is no "divine child abuse" here, as some put it, but abundant suffering on God's part so as to spare us what we deserve.

Yet why doesn't God just forgive us? Why does *anyone* have to suffer at all? When I forgive you, I don't make you suffer. Forgiveness is all about *ending* suffering. Why does God seem to want to make someone suffer, whether us or Jesus?

The first thing to say is that forgiveness in fact always entails suffering. In the case of any non-trivial offense, forgiveness means someone has to suffer. If you have ever forgiven a serious injury, you know how much it hurts to refuse to get even, let alone seek vengeance, and instead to forgive. Striking back is the instinct, to even things out—to "get satisfaction," as the duelists used to say. Refusing to exact one's due means a kind of awful swallowing, an act of self-control and, indeed, self-sacrifice that truly costs the forgiver.

The second thing to say is that the Cross of Jesus Christ is more than just an elaborate, if shocking, symbol of God's self-sacrificial forgiveness. The Cross is more than a grotesque object lesson. The Cross actually solves a problem. It doesn't just point to something else, such as God's love or God's justice. In itself it accomplishes something.

As we have noted already, many of the world's religions speak of wrong actions as affecting the order of things, not just making the gods (or other people, or oneself) unhappy. In India, when individuals fail to do what they should, their negative actions create negative karma. Even more to our point, in tribal societies around the world, breaking tabus—whether one meant to do so or not—creates a bad situation that requires corrective action. Likewise, in the tribal religion of ancient Israel, failing to follow God's law—even in unintentional transgression—broke shalom, damaged the world, and counted as sin. Such transgression required something in return to even things out.

Christianity shares this sense that sin is not only a rupture in our relationships with God and others. Such a relational rupture indeed could be repaired with appropriate repentance and forgive-ness. Sin also, however, somehow makes a mess, incurs a debt, digs a hole, and so on in a range of metaphors that all point to a serious problem in the universe that needs solving, a deficit that needs fil-ling, a wrong that needs righting.

Five-year-old Billy has been given crayons and paper through which to express his burgeoning artistic drive. Mommy sits him in the corner to work away while she finishes drying the dishes. Billy diligently applies himself to his art, but he soon lifts his eyes to spy Mom's heirloom Irish linen tablecloth.

Billy has been told not to color on anything other than his paper. Not the walls, not the floor, and especially not on the tablecloth. But as Billy slowly rises and saunters over to the table, he sees great potential in that tablecloth, at present so boringly white but so won-derfully promising. He therefore climbs up on a chair and goes to work, the call of art drowning out any mere parental proscription.

A shriek interrupts his creative process. Billy looks up to see Mom's horrified face and instantly regrets what he has done. He jumps down, runs to her legs, and throws himself against them in a hug of genuine remorse. Mommy is a far better person and parent than I am, and she quickly drops to her knees to hug and forgive him.

All is well—except for one thing. That tablecloth still needs washing. All of Mommy's goodwill toward Billy won't repair one stroke of his crayons. The relationship of mother and son is restored by repentance and forgiveness. But someone still needs to take care of the damage caused by Billy's sin.

Indeed, the term "forgiveness" includes the idea of repair and restoration. I owe you a thousand dollars. It's time to pay up, but I tell you that I need the money for something else and won't be able to pay you back for some time yet. You compassionately see my side of things, and you decide to forgive the loan, and forgive me. We thus remain friends. But the fact remains that you are out a thousand dollars. Either I pay it, or you do—no matter how we feel about each other. And you have decided to repair the situation by paying yourself, so to speak, the owed money. That's what is entailed in (fully) forgiving a loan.

In the Cross of Christ there is a disorder that is rectified, a stain that is removed, a penalty that is paid, a *something* wrong that is made right by Jesus's sacrifice of himself. The global intuition expressed in tribal cultures from time immemorial is that suffering makes up for, *atones* for, wrong actions.

We see this logic at work in a poignant scene just before Jesus's arrest, trial, and death. In the Garden of Gethsemane just outside Jerusalem, the night before his execution, Jesus confronts his terrible destiny. In an anguished prayer to his Father, Jesus acknowledges that the "cup" of suffering-for-sin must be drained by someone—either by us or by him. However we feel about him and however he feels about us, that is, the wrong must still be righted. Whatever good feelings might obtain on either side, the cup of atonement is still there to be drunk. And Jesus chooses to drink it on our behalf.

The Cross of Christ therefore shows us many splendid things. It exemplifies a hero's commitment to a cause. It assures us of God's love. It inspires devotion. And it marks Christ's victory over all of our enemies, particularly death, hell, and the devil. All of these great things, and more, are important aspects of what Christ accomplishes in the Crucifixion. The Cross of Christ also did what needed to be done, however dimly we can understand it. Jesus suffers—far more than we can imagine, for the suffering due all of us was somehow piled up and dropped on him, the awful pains of scourging and crucifixion being only the outward elements of an inconceivable inner agony.[24] Jesus dies and then literally goes to hell and back for us—for hell, whatever else it is, is the situation in which one makes final atonement for sin.[25]

Jesus then was raised from the dead, this first resurrection signaling both God's endorsement of Jesus as Messiah and the general resurrection to occur at the end of this era (Acts 2:22–36).

After appearing over a few weeks numerous times to his disciples here and there around Jerusalem, Jesus bid them good-bye on the Mount of Olives, just outside Jerusalem. At this time he commissioned them to spread the good news of what God had done; he promised them that the Holy Spirit would come in his place to guide them; and he assured them that he would return one day to make things finally right, once and for all. Then Jesus went straight up into the sky and disappeared into a cloud—an act that symbolized his ascension to the abode of God in heaven, where he would take up his duties as Lord of the Church and Lord of the world.

We have discussed this rich complex of events at the end of Jesus's earthly career—suffering, death, atonement, resurrection, appearances, commissioning, ascension—all too quickly, and it bears long study. For now, however, the point is this: God did the heavy work for us, providing forgiveness for sins (the "negative" part on our inclined plane of salvation), providing rebirth (in the Holy Spirit, the "rebirth" part), and providing the path to sanctification and the power to keep on it (in the ongoing work of the Holy Spirit especially through the Bible and the Church, the "positive" part), with the promise of a final rectification of all things in the Second Coming of Christ. As Trinity, then—as Father-God and Son-God and Spirit-God doing for us what we certainly could not do—would not even want to do—for ourselves, God provided and provides for us what is, in the most fundamental sense, salvation.

What Can Be Done: Our Side

"What shall I return to the Lord for all his bounty to me? I will lift up the cup of salvation and call on the name of the Lord, I will pay my vows to the Lord in the presence of all his people" (Psalm 116:12–14). These verses, buried deep in the Hebrew Bible, nicely sum up the appropriate response of God's people to God's salvation.

First, we wonder at God's generosity. The Supreme Being has loved us—and loved us in extremis. God loved us at the cost of God's own suffering and death for an entire world of sinners. More than that, God has welcomed us into friendship, even *familyhood*—adopting us as sons and daughters, heirs along with the Son of God to the fabulous life of the age to come. More than *that*, God has, in the person of the Holy Spirit, taken up residence in our very hearts, becoming our constant companion. God drew close to Abraham from time to time. God took up residence with Israel in the tabernacle and then the temple. God took on human form and "pitched his tent among us" (John 1:14) in Jesus. And then God the Holy Spirit entered the disciples at the first feast of Pentecost after Jesus's resurrection, indwelling all who believe, in the closest possible form of communion. As preachers sometimes put it, "You can't get closer than *in*."

As believers look, then, at what God has done, is doing, and will do, we ask, What could possibly be an appropriate response to all this? The psalmist has it right. First things first: "I will lift up the cup of salvation and call on the name of the Lord." I will accept the gift God wants to give me—all of it. I will receive salvation and align myself with God. That's what "calling upon the name of the Lord" would mean, as opposed to putting one's trust in (= "calling upon the name of") a different deity, or an alternative philosophy, or one's nation, or oneself. The first appropriate response is to believe and receive.

Stopping there, however, would be to confuse the exchange of marriage vows with the subsequent experience of marriage. Yes, one would be truly married if, immediately after having been pronounced "husband and wife," one fell into a coma. But short of incapacitation, one would expect, and be expected, to take up the identity and duty of a married person. One's spouse gives his or her love and troth for free, but that spouse also rightly expects one's whole life in return to be lived according to the nature of marriage. The obligations of marriage are paralleled by the obligations of adoption. Parents adopt a child without asking the child to pay for the privilege. But those parents then rightly expect the child to act appropriately *as their child*. So with friendship: freely entered into, but then heavy with obligations implicit in the relationship.

The psalmist understands that and continues, "I will pay my vows to the Lord." I will hold up my side of the covenant. Compared to what God has done, is doing, and will do for me, what I have to do is awfully small. But it is also total: I become known as God's, and I act as God's. That's what sanctification—being "set apart for divine use"—literally means.

The Hebrew prophet Micah gives the same train of thought, albeit in extravagant, even shocking, terms:

> With what shall I come before the Lord,
>> and bow myself before God on high?
> Shall I come before him with burnt offerings,
>> with calves a year old?
> Will the Lord be pleased with thousands of rams,
>> with ten thousands of rivers of oil?
> Shall I give my firstborn for my transgression,
>> the fruit of my body for the sin of my soul?
> He has told you, O mortal, what is good;
>> and what does the Lord require of you
> but to do justice, and to love kindness,
>> and to walk humbly with your God? (Micah 6:6–8)

The questioner wonders what in the world he can do to please the Almighty and All-Holy God in the light (or shade) of his many dreadful sins. He begins with the duties laid out in Torah ("burnt offerings") but then quickly amps up his response with "thousands of rams [and] ten thousands of rivers of oil." Since endless sacrifices of animals and plants (olive oil is in view) cannot possibly atone for human sin, he then asks if he should do what other cultures have resorted to when all else has failed to placate the gods: the sacrifice of his own child, the "fruit of my body"—than which no greater sacrifice can be imagined.

The prophet responds in the light of all that God has done, is doing, and will do. Frankly, he implies, you cannot possibly atone for your sin, heal your own disease, and train yourself in right-eousness. Since you are the problem, you cannot be the solution. Christians will say that it is the career of Jesus that fulfills what is only implied here in this Old Testament text. What one must do is what one can do: the right thing (justice), the good thing be-yond the right thing (kindness, generosity, love), and the essential thing ("walk humbly with your God"). For the rest, trust (have faith in) God.

Adam and Eve, however, found that walking the path of life with God in steady determination to do right and eagerness to be gen-erous was too difficult, given the blandishments of evil alternatives. The only two races we know of who have been given free will, angels and humans, both experienced some version of the Fall. So maybe it's simply impossible to keep walking the right way without divine assistance in one's very heart.

Such holiness is certainly impossible for me to maintain on my own. And for you, too. This is why Christianity talks about *conversion*, the changing of something into something else, as requisite for achieving the ultimate good. It will not suffice for us to be told what to do, encouraged what to do, and warned what to do. The do-ers need to be changed, because we are currently incapacitated by sin—so much so that, like seriously ill people who wave away the food they badly need, many of us have lost our appetite for goodness. And even if we're not yet that far gone, we all know that we fall far short of even our own ethical ideals, let alone God's.

We need to be given a rebirth, yes, and a relocation. We need to be given, and trained in, a new spirituality so that we will relate properly to God in prayer, in reading Scripture, in worship, and in other modes of communion with God. We need much more than that, however. We need a new mentality, so that we can reason correctly without our minds being distracted by trivia, driven by ambition, determined by prejudice, or dictated to by illegitimate authority. We need a new morality, so that we judge good and evil rightly and so that we *desire* the good and *hate* the evil with proper intensity. We need a new aesthetic, to discern what is truly beautiful and truly ugly behind what currently might seem only pitiable or impressively glamorous. And we need a new society, a new social location, a new fellowship of like-minded people who can remind us when we forget our convictions, encourage us when we are down, celebrate with us when we succeed, and help us when we falter. Conversion is a big deal: a new mind, a new heart, a new sensibility, and a new community.

Conversion also entails, and not incidentally, a new politics. "Jesus is Lord" is the earliest confession of the earliest Christians, and a direct repudiation of the obligatory slogan, "Caesar is Lord." Caesar is not ignored by the first Christians and their New Testament, but he is put in his place, much like the sun and moon in Genesis 1: as a functionary under the rule of the true Lord, Jesus Christ. He is to be given his due, but only that. Politics, as the art of transacting life together, is ipso facto inescapable, and the Bible doesn't ignore it but deals squarely with it. The first Christians, like Jesus himself, pay their taxes and avoid unnecessary hassles with the authorities. Jesus's famous requirement to "turn the other cheek" is occasioned by the casual abuse of Jews meted out by bullying occupiers (Matthew 5:39–41). Jesus commands his disciples to contribute to shalom by, in a very practical way, forgiving their enemies, taking upon themselves the burden of easing the friction of a fallen world, to make things better by paying debts they do not owe, to be "peacemakers" (Matthew 5:9).[26] Paul tells his churchpeople to bless even the authorities who persecute them, paying due deference to their legitimate (= God-given) authority, and doing all they can "to live in peace with everyone" (Romans 12:14–13:7).

Is this politics then a kind of quietism, a retreat into mysticism from the injustices of the world? No. It is a prioritizing that puts first things first. The Church's fundamental mission is not to revolutionize society. To fully rectify human life is always fundamentally God's work, which God will ultimately accomplish in the Second Coming of Jesus. We, fallen and finite as we are, could never bring about a sinless utopia, and we clearly have never even come close. The Church's fundamental mission is to witness to, exemplify, and help expand the influence of the new life that is available only in Christ through the Holy Spirit. Anything that will help the Church do that is to be embraced, and anything that will hurt the Church's mission is to be avoided.[27]

The politics of the gospel is basically and ultimately revolutionary. Jesus is Lord, not anyone or anything else. When Jesus returns, any rival authority will be completely overthrown. In the interim between Christ's first coming and his second, however, the Plan seems to be for Christians to prioritize spreading the gospel— so that when Jesus does return, the maximum number of people will be on his side and ready to enter the new world ahead. Still, as the gospel transforms lives here and now, those being shaped by the norms of the life of the age to come will bring transformative pressure to bear on social structures here and now—in concert, to be sure, with fellow human beings who retain enough of the image of God to cooperate in such projects of shalom-making.

In the course of Christian civilization, the poor and the sick come to deserve compassion—even from the state.[28] The status of women and children, and of family life itself, is improved. Slavery and patriarchy—almost universal features of human culture— come up for critical review.[29] So do monarchy, and mercantilism, and racial prejudice, and ecological despoliation, and capitalism, and nationalism, and communism, and hedonism, and all idols, all substitute lords, all inadequate alternatives to the reign of Jesus, the kingdom of God. It is not coincidental that these idols have come up for criticism particularly in the one civilization most shaped by

Christianity.[30] Nor is it coincidental that millions of people around the world have been urgently trying to enter the countries whose cultures are most shaped by Christian values—admiring not just our wealth but our ways—while there is precious little reverse traffic.[31]

These huge matters are best pursued in the discourse of Christian ethics. For now, perhaps it is enough to see that the new life brought to us by the Holy Spirit through the work of Jesus begins like a tiny seed in our hearts, a seed of new life that grows up and out into a mature renewal of all things—everything in our own lives, yes, and everything ultimately in the whole world, which is the realization of shalom.

How do Christians foster this new life? They adopt and practice the Christian religion, its beliefs, values, and activities that constitute the way to reconnect themselves and all of life with God. They believe this Story and they believe in this God. They aim to walk with God, conforming their lives to God's intentions, expressed primarily in the Bible—which they take to be the result of God's partnering with select individuals and communities to provide and preserve the inspired text that shapes Christian life across all cultures and eras. They form communities of like-minded people in which they teach to each other, to interested inquirers, to new converts, and to their children the Story, the basic Christian worldview, the sustaining rituals of Christian life, the moral norms of Christian ethics, and the Christ-given mission of the Church. They thus explain, exemplify, and extend to others the new life available in Jesus through the Holy Spirit, the life of the age to come.

Over time, under the Providential work of God, the Problem is being solved. Revelation both of the great God and of perfect human life has been given to us in Christ; atonement has been made in his suffering and death; new life has been provided in his resurrection and the coming of the Holy Spirit; inspired guidance has been granted through the writing and transmission of the Bible; and sustaining fellowship has been established through the founding and spread of the Church. Little by little, person by person, family by family, and tribe by tribe, the good news has been spreading, and its implications have transformed more and more of human life around the world.

"God was in Christ reconciling the world to himself," as the Christian Scriptures proclaim (2 Corinthians 5:19). Here is the solution to the world's fundamental crisis. Here is the fulfillment of our every proper longing. Here is the Answer.

In Jesus of Nazareth. The carpenter turned rabbi. The man recognized by no legitimate authority of his time, whether political or religious, but rather eliminated as a mere nuisance by the provincial powers he unnerved. This victim on a cross is the Winner of the World. This man about whom so many strange stories are told and to whom so many strange sayings are attributed is the Final Way, Truth, and Life of all humanity. This figure whose supposed divine validation comes from a resurrection witnessed only patchily by a few over a fortnight or two is the One upon whom all human history depends and in whom all humanity should put their truth for everything and forevermore.

Really?

One might grant that the story has its own odd coherence, that the Christian construals of problem and solution do line up, and that a certain amount of admirable progress has been made, it seems, in the wake of the spread of Christianity. Yet what about Christianity's implication in imperialism, forced or enticed conversion, disrespect for native traditions, hypocrisy, small-mindedness, and stupidity?[32] Has the Christian religion been a good thing for humanity, even on the whole? Moreover, the outlandishness of the story remains. This crucified man, long ago and far away, is the Answer and Savior and Lord of the world? How could anyone believe it? How could anyone trust it?

How could *two billion people* or more—some of them, at least, to all appearances both sane and intelligent—trust it? Well, let's see.

3

Why Does Anyone Believe?

Let's be clear about what we're going to do in this chapter. We are about to survey the range of various grounds on which various Christians and various Christian communities have variously found their religion to be credible. Not every believer or church would rely on every one of these grounds, but they are the ones that show up most often in the Christian record.

These grounds have been extensively defended by Christians over the centuries, often at book length—and critics have responded in kind. We cannot possibly set them all out here in even an approximately full way. All we can hope to do is to sketch their outlines, to provide an introduction to "how they go." We're walking through a gallery, not studying each item in all its complexity. But, as a responsible guide, I can indicate where the interested person can go for more information, and I do so in the notes.

So let's begin the tour.

Since Christianity Focuses on Christ

The world offers us many religious varieties—and let's keep in mind that by "religious" we include Big Explanations of All Sorts by Which People Live (ideologies, philosophies, religions, worldviews), according to our *functional* definition of religion. They not only differ in obvious ways, from costume to language to myth to art and ritual. They differ in basic kind.

Buddhism commends its answer to the world's problems without much concern for whether the stories told about the career of the Buddha are literally true—indeed, whether or not there even was a historic character Siddhartha who achieved Enlightenment. Some Buddhists cheerfully doubt it, while many others focus on different buddhas and bodhisattvas entirely. The point of Buddhism (the mainstream Theravada and Mahayana varieties) is whether it *works* to eliminate suffering. It is, to use its own favorite image, merely a *vehicle*, and if the vehicle gets you where you want to go—namely, achieving a particular attitude toward reality—then it has achieved its sole purpose. Whether a former prince ever sat under a tree in northwest India in ancient times and became enlightened doesn't finally matter. Have *you* achieved enlightenment? That's what matters.

The same is true in Hinduism regarding the famous tales told about Rama or Krishna or Shiva or Deva. As most gurus make clear (again, generalizations about Hinduism are always vulnerable to exceptions!), these great stories are not meant to be taken as accounts of actual historical occurrences, even if many devotees do take them as such—hence the shrines all over India to mark the very place in which Rama did this or Krishna did that. The main *function* of the myths is to illustrate fundamental truths regarding ultimate reality so as to guide people in their dharma—and perhaps along one of the margas ("ways") that promise to release one from the wheel of reincarnation. If you're doing what you're supposed to be doing and achieving what there is to achieve, all is well. Whether Krishna or Rama actually visited this spot is wildly off the point.

Confucian wisdom is understood to be wise on its own merits, not on the authority of ancient Chinese sages such as Kongzi (Confucius) and Mengzi, whose authorship of much that has been attributed to them is in doubt. Daoism rests on the writings of figures such Laozi and Zhuangzi, who are judged by some scholars to be mythical, and this judgment is made without any cost to the vitality of Daoism. Even in Islam, similar as it is in some respects to

Christianity, what finally matters is not the career of Muhammad. What matters centrally is the authenticity of the Qur'an as the very speech of God. The pattern of Muhammad's life established the normative pattern for all Muslim devotion, and thus details from his life of his sayings and doings do matter a good deal. As highly as the Prophet is venerated, however, Islam warns against anything approaching worship of any human being. God alone is to be praised and honored as supreme, and the truth of Islam rests in the truth of its scripture as the Word of God, not of any of its prophets.

No other world religion makes the same claim regarding history that Christianity does. Not even Judaism, deeply rooted as it is in the historical event of the Exodus as the basis for Israel's faithfulness to Yhwh. "I am Yhwh your God who brought you out of the land of Egypt, out of the house of slavery: You shall have no other gods ahead of me" is the way the Ten Commandments begin (Exodus 20:2–3). The Christian faith depends *completely* upon what God accomplished in the career of Jesus of Nazareth—in that man, in that place, in that time. The validity of the whole Christian Story depends entirely on whether Jesus of Nazareth really did die, really did rise from the dead, and really did ascend into heaven as the world's Savior and Lord.

The situation is as radical as this: if someone could somehow produce the bones of Jesus today with convincing evidence for identifying them as such, classical Christianity would collapse. Likewise, if one could demonstrate the historical baselessness of the Gospels, and particularly their accounts of the suffering, death, resurrection, and ascension of Jesus (as many people have attempted to do, especially in the last three hundred years), then some sort of religion might remain and it might be called "Christianity," but it would no longer be anything close to the faith of the historic Church.[1]

This distinctive emphasis upon historicity does not add any particular luster to the Christian religion over others. Indeed, some people over the years have seen this emphasis on the singular story of a singular individual to be strong prima facie evidence against the universal claims of Christianity: How can something that is supposed to be globally relevant be so peculiarly particular? This question will nag us into the final chapter. For now, however, we begin accounting for the phenomenon of Christian faith—Why do so many people find this very odd story to be a convincing explanation of things?—on grounds appropriate to that faith: namely, historical grounds.

Christians believe not only that Jesus was an important historical personage (as most people do) or that Jesus was in fact a prophet of God (as Muslims and Baha'is also do), but that Jesus was and is the actual human face of God: God in human form. As we have seen, Christians affirm the peculiar doctrine of the Trinity chiefly because they believe that in the historical figure of Jesus of Nazareth they see God—not just messages from God, or the love of God, or even "godliness," but *God*. And so, to the bewilderment and even scandalization of people of other outlooks, Christians do not merely respect or even revere Jesus, but they worship him as divine—without extending that status to any other person or being. Christians, like Jews, Muslims, and Sikhs, are fierce monotheists. But the one God of Christianity exists in three persons: Father, Son (now in heaven), and the Holy Spirit (who indwells each believer, and the Church as a whole, and connects them spiritually with Jesus).

The dazzling prospect of knowing God in Jesus through communing with the Holy Spirit, however, depends upon a satisfactory answer to the fundamental historical question: Is it true that Jesus was, and is, God in human form? What intellectually persuasive warrants can be offered for this assertion? Moreover, for Christians Jesus is not only a divine figure. He described himself as "the Son of Man," and he functions for Christians as the new Adam, the properly functioning human being who is the Great Example of how to live well with God, each other, and the rest of creation. If Jesus did not exist, or if the accounts we have of his life are not trustworthy, we lose this portrait of the Good Life, this perfect model of doing justice, loving kindness, and walking humbly with God.

The historical reliability of the Bible's portrayal of Jesus, therefore, is simply foundational to Christianity. Without it, Christianity at best becomes something else, if it does not disappear into dust.

What, then, are the historical grounds upon which Christians have placed their trust in the New Testament, and thus in Jesus?

Historical Grounds

For several years I taught a standard university survey course on the history of Western civilization. Eventually we would arrive at the origins of the Christian religion, and I would dutifully relate a simple version of the career of Jesus of Nazareth and of the ideas and practices of the early church. It was literally textbook stuff.

After teaching this course a few times, however, I began to dread the arrival of this particular unit in the course. It dawned on me that a keen and persistent student could make things awkward for me by asking a single particular question. Let's imagine the situation.

I have just finished my presentation on the history of early Christianity. I ask for questions and comments, and a keen and persistent student puts up her hand.

"Professor Stackhouse," she asks politely, "did Jesus rise from the dead?"

With my customary poise I smile and smoothly reply, "Carolyn, I trust I made it clear that the early church did believe and proclaim that Jesus had risen from the dead. This is a foundational belief in the New Testament and indeed in all subsequent Christianity." I beam at her and then look around for the next question.

Carolyn, undaunted by my condescension, patiently continues. "Yes, I understood that. Thank you, sir. But my question is not about the beliefs of Jesus's followers. It is about Jesus himself. You have told us in this course that Julius Caesar crossed the Rubicon in 44 BC and by that act initiated the fall of the Roman Republic. You have told us that Jerusalem was leveled by the Romans in AD 70 as a devastating reprisal after a Jewish uprising. When you discussed these events, you didn't say that 'Romans believed this happened' or 'Jews believed that happened,' but that these two events just plain happened. So I am asking you, did the resurrection of Jesus actually happen?"

I now am stuck, wriggling on the horns of a trilemma. First, if Jesus of Nazareth really did rise from the dead, then it becomes much more likely that other key elements of the Christian proclamation, which are not so amenable to historical investigation, would be true as well. The resurrection would vindicate Jesus's work and word. It would follow that this historical event is, in fact, the most important single event in world history. So how can I, as a professional historian, not venture an opinion on whether it happened?

Second, if Jesus of Nazareth did not rise from the dead, then the Christian religion stems from a huge and fundamental misunderstanding, if not a terrible deception. Given Christianity's stupendous global impact, this assertion, in its turn, would be the most important single (non-)event in world history, leaving a gigantic hole at the origin of the world's largest social movement. So how can I, as a professional historian, not venture an opinion on whether it happened?

Third, suppose that I want to avoid plunging my class into controversy, and so I refuse to offer a judgment on the matter. Suppose I retreat into what I'd like to think is a fair-minded agnosticism, claiming only to conclude from the available historical evidence that *Christians believed* that Jesus rose from the dead, but also that there is no way to ascertain with appropriate historiographical rigor whether he actually did so from our critical vantage point.

Alas, I owe the student a straight answer. For from the earliest Christian sermons to those of the present, Christianity claims that God vindicated Jesus by raising him from the dead; that human hope for a general resurrection in the future depends upon this particular resurrection in the past; and that without belief in the actual, historical resurrection of Jesus, the Christian faith falls to ashes—since Christianity is all about what God *does* in history, not about timeless spiritual or ethical principles.

The apostle Peter, in what the New Testament depicts as the first public address of the Christian church, stood up in the midst of a Jewish festival in Jerusalem, scant weeks after the execution of Jesus in that city, and boldly cried out,

> You that are Israelites, listen to what I have to say: Jesus of Nazareth, a man attested to you by God with deeds of power, wonders, and signs that God did through him among you, as you yourselves know—this man, handed over to you according to the definite plan and foreknowledge of God, you crucified and killed by the hands of those outside the law. But God raised him up, having freed him from death, because it was impossible for him to be held in its power. (Acts 2:22–24)

Peter links Jesus with the ancient hero King David, claiming that David himself prophesied the resurrection of the Messiah (or "Christ"). Peter pounds his point home:

> This Jesus God raised up, and of that all of us are witnesses. Being therefore exalted at the right hand of God, and having received from the Father the promise of the Holy Spirit, he has poured out this that you both see and hear. For David did not ascend into the heavens, but he himself says, "The Lord [God] said to my Lord [Messiah], 'Sit at my right hand, until I make your enemies your footstool.'" Therefore let the entire house of Israel know with certainty that God has made him both Lord and Messiah, this Jesus whom you crucified. (Acts 2:32–36)

Peter thus answers the skeptic's question: Why does God raise *this* person from the dead and not everybody? Why not a Great Big

Universal Miracle instead of this particular, peculiar one? The answer lies chiefly in Jesus's unique and supremely important identity and role. *This one*, who was cruelly tortured and dispensed with as a misguided, misguiding nuisance to the powers that be, is in fact God's Self-Expression, the Exemplary Human, and the Savior of the World. And God has demonstrated Jesus's uniqueness and supreme importance precisely by raising *him* from the dead *and not (yet) anyone else.*

From Peter we can turn to the apostle Paul, another pillar of first-century Christianity. In one of his earliest extant letters to a Christian church, Paul identifies the gospel itself with belief in the resurrection of Jesus:

> Now I would remind you, brothers and sisters, of the good news that I proclaimed to you, which you in turn received, in which also you stand, through which also you are being saved, if you hold firmly to the message that I proclaimed to you—unless you have come to believe in vain. For I handed on to you as of first importance what I in turn had received: that Christ died for our sins in accordance with the scriptures, and that he was buried, and that he was raised on the third day in accordance with the scriptures, and that he appeared to Cephas [the Aramaic form of "Peter"], then to the twelve [disciples]. Then he appeared to more than five hundred brothers and sisters at one time, most of whom are still alive, though some have died. Then he appeared to James, then to all the apostles. Last of all, as to one untimely born, he appeared also to me. (1 Corinthians 15:1–8)

Paul goes on to deal with an erroneous teaching apparently present in the church to which he writes, namely, that there is no resurrection of the dead. Paul replies to this idea with vehemence that becomes repetitive as he won't let go of the crucial doctrine of the resurrection—both that of Jesus in the past, and of believers in the future:

Now if Christ is proclaimed as raised from the dead, how can some of you say there is no resurrection of the dead? If there is no resurrection of the dead, then Christ has not been raised; and if Christ has not been raised, then our proclamation has been in vain and your faith has been in vain. We are even found to be misrepresenting God, because we testified of God that he raised Christ—whom he did not raise if it is true that the dead are not raised. For if the dead are not raised, then Christ has not been raised. If Christ has not been raised, your faith is futile and you are still in your sins. Then those also who have died in Christ have perished. If for this life only we have hoped in Christ, we are of all people most to be pitied. But [Paul concludes] in fact Christ has been raised from the dead. (1 Corinthians 15:12–20)

If I, as a professor of history, can offer to my class only the judgment that the resurrection of Jesus is a belief of the early church that cannot be judged historically one way or another, then I am asserting that—despite Christianity's claims to be founded on something that actually happened and can be known to have happened—the whole Christian religion is instead founded upon radical historical uncertainty. And *that* in itself might be the most important single fact of world history.

I cannot avoid deciding about the purported resurrection of Jesus. Nor can any thoughtful person giving even a cursory glance at the Christian faith. It turns out that the resurrection of Jesus is not the kind of matter toward which one can shrug, as many understandably would be inclined to do at first blush. Instead, the question of Jesus's resurrection becomes an unshakable intellectual burr for anyone who takes the time to look at it clearly.

Let us abandon me in my nightmarish classroom, skewered by Carolyn's intellectual honesty and unsure which tack to take, and move on to consider a positive response. What warrants can Christianity adduce for what seems to be a preposterous claim: not just that something or someone somehow resuscitated Jesus following his apparent death (after all, don't EMTs do this every day?), but that three days after his execution, Jesus appeared to his followers not as a candidate for an intensive care unit but as the glorious conqueror of death and the inspiring harbinger of eternal life? Answering the question must proceed in two stages. We will consider, of course, the data that Christians believe point to the fact of Jesus's resurrection. But before examining this evidence, we must ascertain the reliability of the sources for these data.

Our main source of information about the career of Jesus is, of course, the New Testament. Some Christian apologists point also to references to the life and death of Jesus that appear in other ancient sources, such as the Jewish historian Josephus and the Roman writer Suetonius. But precious little can be gleaned from such sources beyond the brute fact of Jesus's life and its termination by the Roman authorities in Judea. Not surprisingly, the only ancient writers who took seriously any details about the life and death of an obscure religious leader in a backwater of the Roman Empire were those writers who believed that he was in truth the Son of God.

We are confined, then, to evidently biased sources: writers who believe the truth of what they describe and, much more worrisome, are committed to the religion that emerged from those events. Isn't the situation hopeless, therefore, before we even begin?

No, it isn't. The Gospel writers' adherence to Christianity does not necessarily disqualify them as reliable sources of information. No historian devotes time and energy to a subject that does not interest him or about which he does not form strong opinions. Herodotus and Thucydides, the classical Greek "fathers of history," show obvious biases and not-so-hidden agendas in works that we nonetheless prize for their descriptions of the ancient world. Julius Caesar was scarcely a disinterested observer of the Roman conquest of ancient France, but his account of the Gallic Wars nonetheless stands as our only important account of those events, and historians have taken it seriously for centuries. Crucial historical material constantly emerges from people with strong views about the matters they discuss, and important historical sources are ipso facto often people who participated in, or at least were very close to, the events they describe. (Think of the memoirs turned out by people who have just left high government office or the executive suite of major corporations. Do we junk them all as historically useless?) The critical question with respect to any account is not whether the writer has a particular opinion on his theme (for all writers do), or whether the writer is proximate to the events he describes (as if that would somehow be a bad thing, rather than an advantage), or whether the author is somehow personally invested in his subject, but instead whether the writer offers reasonable and adequate evidence for his conclusions.

Consider some everyday examples. Football fans can give accurate accounts of games they have seen, even those involving their favorite teams. We count on critics to render fair-minded descriptions of works they finally like or dislike. Even sportsmen may (sometimes) offer a dependable account of just how big was the fish that got away. When listening to such accounts, an intelligent person rightly recognizes the bias of the source to see whether and how that bias distorts the account. An intelligent person does not, however, discount her sources simply because they are interested in what they are describing. After all, most people interested in a subject—any subject, great or small—have opinions about it that affect, but do not necessarily compromise the veracity of, their representation of it.

This point may need a little more reinforcement, since the dismissive retort, "Well, they're just biased," seems so common. Philosopher C. A. J. Coady has thought a lot about the reliability of testimony, and in his modern classic on the subject he says this about our present concern—namely, about whether we should trust only the testimony of witnesses who have no interest in the subject about which they speak:

Very few actual people, if any, fit such a characterization. There are, of course, impartial people but they are not necessarily people who have nothing to gain from, or no interest in, the outcome of an inquiry, but rather people whose interest in and concern for the truth dominates whatever other interest they have in the proceedings. It may be doubted whether there are any "outsiders" whose interest in the proceeding is so neutral that no description of it can be found which will rank, in the abstract, as a factor tending to bias. The most neutral observer is liable to have an interest in having his general outlook on the world, or certain aspects of it, reinforced by what he has experienced and this can lead to dramatic error. . . .

. . . The disadvantages that may arise from the partiality of an interest may be counterbalanced by the disadvantages that lack of interest may create. After all, a strong interest in some issue makes one pay a lot of attention to what is going on; the attention may be biased by the strength of the interest but the observation will not suffer from the dangers attendant upon casual concern. Lack of a strong interest in the issue or the outcome is liable to produce unfocused attention and lack of detailed observation. Roughly speaking, testimony can fail either through deceit or mistake and if partiality mostly induces deceit, indifference mostly induces mistake or inaccuracy.[2]

Matthew, Mark, Luke, and John—understood by ancient church tradition to be the Gospel authors—were not professional historians. They came from four different trades: Matthew was a tax collector, Luke was a physician, John was a fisherman, and we don't know Mark's occupation. Like almost all ancient historians, each was an amateur doing his best to present his readers with a reliable account of something of common concern.[3] The four Gospel writers worked the same way all historians do. They collected accounts, both oral and written; they reflected on those accounts in the light of whatever personal experience they might have had with their subject; and they wrote about their subject in a way they hoped would be interesting and useful for their intended audiences.

But did they write reliable history? To answer this honestly, I need to risk making enemies among my academic friends. I know of no field of contemporary literary or historical study that is as rich, but also as confused, as New Testament scholarship. Philosophers like to say that they argue about everything, but they actually don't, and when they do have at each other they generally take up the cudgels cheerfully and with good-natured zest for the next go-round. New Testament scholars, however, seem locked in perpetual life-and-death battles between their own obvious, clear-as-day logic on one side and the bigoted obscurantism of the other side. Indeed, it seems that one can find a well-credentialed scholar proclaiming virtually any thesis imaginable about this or that part of the New Testament.

There are a variety of reasons for this cacophony of dissenting voices. For one thing, no text in Western civilization matters as much as the New Testament: not the dialogues of Plato, not the Magna Charta, not the plays of Shakespeare, not the Declaration of Independence, not Einstein's papers on relativity. For better or worse, no text has affected our civilization like this collection of small first-century books. So it matters a lot what we think it says— regardless of whether it is true and good or not. Furthermore, when scholars study the New Testament, ultimate things are at stake. The text claims to describe the most fundamental realities: God, the world, humanity, sin, salvation, heaven, hell, morality. And billions of people have believed it. Who then can study it and remain indifferent to its implications?

While we can recognize the erudition of many New Testament scholars past and present, therefore, it is simply predictable (and, I think, evident) that in at least some cases their expertise has been put at the service of personal religious agendas. In the eighteenth and nineteenth centuries, pioneering scholars such as Reimarus, Wellhausen, and Baur pursued their studies with openly unorthodox, even anti-orthodox, concerns that skewed their work—even as each of them made important contributions to the understanding of the Bible. There is no reason to suppose that contemporary scholars are different from their distinguished predecessors.[4]

The scholarly voices that find the Gospels suspect as historical sources must be listened to with as much caution as those who say otherwise, particularly since many reputable scholars do say otherwise. One must neither accept unquestioningly whatever happens to be the trend of the moment in New Testament scholarship nor wash one's hands of the whole field entirely. A critical arm's-length stance serves one well in any area of human inquiry, and especially in one so contested as this.

Mainstream Christians have concluded that the Gospels are at least basically reliable in their portrayals of Jesus. The Gospels (and, to the extent that they describe Jesus, the epistles also) vary from each other in details, even important ones, but their individual and composite portraits of the life and times of Jesus of Nazareth seem at least as reliable as any other historical sources we have about the ancient world. For one thing, there are four main accounts: not one or two, as is often the case with classical sources. And these accounts agree with each other far more than they seem to disagree. Some skeptics have attempted to attribute this agreement to collusion among the four writers, but this seems a rather desperate tack. Some Christians have argued that it seems silly to level a charge of massive deceit against devotees of a religious master whom everyone agrees taught honesty as a supreme virtue. (It would be a different thing, for instance, to suspect propagandistic collusion among Nazi biographers of Hitler.) Still, apparently devoted Christians have, through the centuries, perpetrated lots of evil in the name of Christ. Perhaps more persuasive is the fact that the very differences among the four Gospels to which other critics enjoy pointing make a conspiracy of agreement highly unlikely. It would be a poor conspiracy that so obviously failed to iron out the many differences among the Gospels. The more sensible, because straightforward, explanation for our having four different, but mutually reinforcing, accounts is that they are describing the same reality from four different and variously informed points of view.

These accounts agree with each other far more than they do with other gospels written in the early centuries: those attributed to the apostles Thomas and Peter, for example, or the early missionary Barnabas. The early churches quickly latched onto the four Gospels that became part of the New Testament—in church after church across the empire, as archaeology has shown—while repudiating others as fanciful, even heretical. This widespread agreement on the status of the four Gospels over against their "competitors," an agreement noted by scholars of various stripes, is a phenomenon not to be dismissed lightly, especially in the light of modern excitement over so-called Gnostic and other much later gospels that present very different versions of Jesus. The early churches ought to be treated as the best judges of which gospels got the story right. Why?

Eyewitnesses to Jesus's life were still alive at the time of the writing and circulation of the Gospels, and these eyewitnesses could easily and authoritatively have refuted, and did refute, any phony account. Written within the lifetimes of the first generation after Jesus (between AD 50 and 100, with the death of Jesus dated at about 30), the four Gospels of the New Testament were accepted quickly and widely by the generation that had been taught the "Jesus traditions" by the apostles themselves. The vast majority of the early churches—and we have records right back to the late first century—broadly and independently agreed that these four accounts were authentic, that they give reliable reports of what actually happened.

So while scholars argue over whether Luke has a particular historical reference correct or whether John is putting words into the mouth of Jesus that he never said, we might sensibly consider one thing that New Testament scholars rarely dispute. *The early Christians themselves* adopted these four as their basic community remembrances of the life of their Lord. The early churches prized these four accounts because, in their view, they told the truth about Jesus.[5]

Many of the elements of Jesus's career upon which all four Gospel writers agree are also mentioned in the still-earlier letters of the apostle Paul, which were written in the 50s and 60s, within only a few decades of Jesus's death. And these New Testament letters also—at least the major ones, such as Romans and 1 and 2 Corinthians—were early on received by most churches as teaching the truth about Jesus. So we in fact have five sources, all written within a century of the events they purport to describe, that might disagree on details but massively agree on the essential elements of Jesus's life, from which emerges a remarkable, and remarkably consistent, personality. How could that be so if they were not describing, and at least fairly accurately, the same person? These five sources together constitute an impressively rich, coherent, and reliable base for study, especially when compared with any other records from the classical period of Greco-Roman history. In sum, if we apply to the New Testament documents the same tests that professional historians normally apply to other ancient accounts, we clearly have at least as much reason to trust the Gospels as sources of historical data about Jesus as we do to trust any other writer, writing about any other subject, in the ancient Mediterranean world.

Some people are troubled by our temporal distance from these events. It all happened so long ago. Couldn't something, or lots of things, have happened in the meanwhile that might have corrupted the history, or the texts, so that all we have now is what the (later) Church wants us to think happened?

Again, let's just apply the same thinking we would apply to any other question of ancient history. Regarding the sheer passage of time, do we really have less reason to be confident of the existence of, say, Plato (d. 348 BC) or Julius Caesar (d. 44 BC) than did Marcus Aurelius, the second-century emperor and philosopher who doubtless was interested in them both? With all we know now about the ancient world through the accumulation of evidence and centuries of painstaking investigation, aren't we in some respects *more* knowledgeable about Plato and Julius Caesar than was Marcus Aurelius? And as for the transmission of the Bible over the centuries, sensationalist conspiracy theories—such as that the early church was a maelstrom of wildly conflicting views and writings eventually sorted out only under the heavy hand of Emperor Constantine and his successors—just aren't true to the facts. The chain of manuscripts that we now possess, thousands of them, go back to the second century and even possibly the first. We know better. Indeed, the Biblical text we have today is likely closer to what was circulated among the early Christians than was available until our time.[6]

Having said all this—and that's quite a lot to say—even if one takes a minimalist approach to the historicity of the Gospel accounts, even if one grants merely for the sake of argument that the Gospels contain a large number of minor inaccuracies, or even, again for sake of argument, if one concedes that the Gospels contain major mistakes or fabrications (Christians typically do not believe that such major discrepancies exist)—one confronts affirmations in all four Gospels that are crucial, not incidental, events in the narratives.

Let's pare even *these* affirmations down to just two facts, and two facts that, let it be clear, are not in themselves miraculous. Grant these two and let's see what else might reasonably follow.

The two facts are these: (1) an empty tomb and (2) convinced disciples.

After his death by crucifixion, Jesus was buried in a tomb owned by a secret follower, Joseph of Arimathea. Jesus's tomb was a cave sealed with a rolling rock of some sort. The four Gospels record many, many details of Jesus's death, burial, and resurrection, but for the present purpose almost all of those details can be set aside as we focus on just one: the empty tomb.

Each of the four Gospels records that it was found to be empty (save for Jesus's graveclothes). Now, perhaps the Gospels are mistaken or dishonest about this assertion of a vacant grave. If so, then why, when rumors of Jesus's resurrection began to circulate in ancient Jerusalem, did neither the Jewish nor the Roman authorities (neither group being friends of Jesus or his followers) simply go to the tomb and produce the body? For that matter, why didn't any skeptic simply find out where Jesus had been buried and investigate the situation? In fact, given the speed of decomposition, even taking into account ancient Jewish embalming practices, wouldn't *any* body have sufficed at least to throw a shadow of doubt over the disciples' startling claim? Given the emphasis that early Christian preachers were placing upon the resurrection of Jesus, the public production of his corpse would have smothered Christianity in its cradle. It seems much more likely, therefore, that the Gospel accounts are correct in their assertion that, for whatever reason, the tomb was empty.

Perhaps Jesus's body was not in the tomb because he had revived and escaped. Modern movies are full of heroes (and villains) who appear to have died, even brutally, but then reappear, somehow having had the strength to survive. This explanation, however, faces considerable obstacles.

First, why would the Roman executioners, skilled in their terrible craft, be mistaken about Jesus's condition and allow him to be taken out of their custody while still alive? It would have cost them dearly to have failed in their simple, if dreadful, task of killing this enemy of the state.

Second, given the wounds from the flogging Jesus suffered from the Roman soldiers at Pilate's behest, and the injuries he then incurred in the crucifixion itself, how likely is it that Jesus would be healthier after a number of hours in the tomb than he was when he was placed there? How much more likely is it that, even if he had been placed in the tomb alive, he would have soon died from exposure or loss of blood? Perhaps, in fact, the soldiers didn't much care whether Jesus was quite dead when they handed his body over to his followers, but that was because they would have known his beating before the crucifixion plus his agony during it would have sufficed to finish him off before long. These men, who dealt in death all the time, were satisfied that this victim, too, was gone—or would be soon.

Third, the graveclothes in which Jesus was wrapped, if they were typical of the time (and why would they not be?), would have been made of linen fiber, which is extraordinarily difficult to break. In the custom of the time, Jesus's body would have been wrapped tightly from neck to foot, with a separate cloth for the head. Even a professional escape artist would find such a predicament daunting, but a victim of crucifixion freeing himself from such encumbrances is a preposterous scenario.

Still, is it not possible that a barely alive Jesus could have been elaborated into a later myth of triumphant resurrection? Aside from the medical facts we have been discussing, we face now a kind of anthropological problem: such a myth would have had much too little time to form. Few scholars doubt that Jesus was crucified sometime around AD 30, and most agree that Paul wrote to the Christians in the Greek city of Corinth (hence the New Testament letters known as 1 and 2 Corinthians) about the resurrection fewer than thirty years later. Within a generation of Jesus's death, that is, his resurrection was being taught by Paul and others as standard Christian doctrine. As social scientists and literary scholars recognize, myths that make extraordinary claims, especially supernatural ones, that go on to shape whole communities usually take a lot longer than that to form: centuries, not a couple of decades.

Let's be clear that we're not talking about mere "miracle stories." Those can jump up anywhere at any time. We're talking about a certain kind of *myth*: a story that morphs from what is understood at the time *not* to have happened to what a later community asserts *did* happen, whether in the form of extravagant elaboration (an odd event turns into a spectacular wonder) or a completely different occurrence (a dead man becomes a live man). There has to be a considerable interval between the original event—and everyone who knew what actually happened—and the myth taking hold of a community such that the mists of time lend the latter story a credibility that couldn't possibly be granted the story at the time of its occurrence. No, there wasn't time for *that* sort of thing to happen here.

The proposal of myth-making, moreover, begs the question as to whether this particular group of disciples were likely candidates for an enterprise of this sort. Is this the kind of group that could be expected to trade in outlandish ideas such as the resurrection of their leader? As Jews, they might have hoped for a general resurrection at the end of time, during which all would stand before God in final judgment. But, as scholars of Jewish religion tell us, precisely no one was expecting or even hoping for the resurrection of a single individual while the rest of history moved on as ever. The Gospels make it clear that the disciples themselves, despite Jesus's own hints to the contrary while he was alive, were not expecting to see him again. As far as they all knew, he was dead and gone. So on what grounds would one imagine that this group somehow became convinced of a completely novel idea: that Jesus was, singularly, alive again?

It could be, of course, that something else was going on and the disciples engaged in a different sort of plot entirely. Perhaps they themselves purloined the dead body of Jesus precisely in order to foment the idea of resurrection. Should we suspect them of mendacity, rather than credulity? To what plausible end would they have perpetuated this fraud, a fraud that cost many of them their livelihood, freedom, and life itself? As Todd Lake points out, "The earliest followers of Jesus were devout Jews. They knew they would suffer death here and damnation in the hereafter for lying about God's actions and proclaiming a false, dead Messiah to their contemporaries."[7]

A third alternative is that the disciples weren't especially credulous, nor were they duplicitous, but instead they somehow all hallucinated—separately in some instances and together in others—such that they came to sincerely believe their master was alive when in fact he was dead. Now we're really stretching, aren't we?[8]

Whichever of the three options one selects, one must deal with the second main datum to be explained: the extraordinary attitude and actions of the disciples after Jesus's reported resurrection.

The Gospels portray the disciples almost all as cowards during Jesus's arrest, trial, and execution. Given the widespread Jewish belief of the time that the Messiah would return in divine power to destroy precisely the Gentile oppressors who were now crushing Jesus, it is entirely understandable that the disciples were thrown into a confusion of terror and despair. The Gospels tell us only what we would expect to hear about such followers at such a time. What needs to be explained is the subsequent confidence of such followers in such a terrifically unlikely story: that the leader of their little band had in fact been raised to new life by God and had empowered them to bring the good news of his victory over evil to the entire world. Zeal was one thing, perhaps commendable in a land with little hope of freedom. But ancient Jews, according to what cultural records we have, were not more credulous about such matters than most of us are today. Resurrection was the hope of some, yes, but as a general reality to be enjoyed by all of God's people only after the Last Judgment and in the Messianic kingdom to follow. One lone resurrection as the divine vindication of a crucified Messiah seemed an utter contradiction in terms, and organized Judaism soon moved to stamp out any such idea as a completely preposterous, even scandalous, misunderstanding of Jewish religion. The Christian Jews, however, persisted in their assertion that Jesus was indeed raised from the dead and that God had raised him so as to vindicate his status and his message as Messiah. Many of those Christians went on to lose careers, families, and even their lives for their faithfulness to this one message: God raised Jesus from the dead, and one day God will raise you, too, if you will believe.

Let's be blunt. Perhaps the disciples were liars and made up the whole thing. They would have had to have persisted in a large and sustained conspiracy, lasting decades, without a single one of them admitting the truth of what actually happened. Furthermore, since it is likely that at least some of the ancient traditions about their deaths are true, then some of the apostles died, and died violently, for what they must have known to be untrue. How likely is that?

At some point, surely at least one of them would have blown the whistle to save himself or his family. Even if all of the traditions about their martyrdoms are untrue, however, what motive would the earliest Christians have for teaching such a thing? They did not attempt to seize political power by exploiting this story. There was no commercial angle to be played, no money to be made. They certainly did not enjoy greater esteem from their fellows, Jewish or Gentile, but quite the contrary: they were suspect at best and persecuted at worst. Indeed, they quite directly risked suffering the same terrible fate as Jesus's at the hands of the very same powers. They gained only a few thousand converts for the first several decades, to no discernible profit. *Why would they lie?*

One thinks in stark contrast of the rather rapid unraveling of conspiracies in our own era, whether Nixon's Watergate co-conspirators failing to keep quiet for even a fortnight, Reagan's Iran-Contra scandal emerging quickly into the full light of a con-gressional inquiry, and Trump's many transgressions being exposed by one former colleague after another. And most of these people had only (!) money, power, and prestige to preserve and a relatively mild prison term to avoid. Jesus's disciples willingly endured arrest, torture, and death—and not one of them cracked.

So it seems virtually impossible that they lied. But perhaps they were deluded. Again how likely is this possibility? How big a mistake can a large and growing group of people make, and keep making? In fact, it wasn't just one mistake they were making, for the resurrection of Jesus carried direct implications that were evident throughout the early sermons of the Church—namely, that Yhwh raised Jesus from the dead in order to vindicate his life, teaching, and work in toto. So how did this whole group of disciples become convinced of the success of a cause and a person who had, according to the standards of their own culture, apparently been an utter failure? Did they simply make up the reports of appearances of Jesus (such as those cited by Paul in the letter quoted earlier), or did they actually have such experiences as figments of wishful thinking? Did they all possess such powerful imaginations—imaginations, let us remain blunt, that in this case crossed over into sustained psychosis—that they believed that they had seen Jesus, talked with Jesus, touched Jesus, and been commissioned by Jesus to convert the entire world before his ascent to heaven? These are grand, or grandiose, beliefs indeed. Furthermore, did they do so with apparently no dispute about these matters among the central core of followers, even as the historical records show that the early church disagreed about many other, much less critical and dangerous matters?

Again, to be as careful as possible here, we can allow that it remains at least logically possible that the whole thing was a massive exercise in group fabrication of an intentional or unintentional sort. Airtight proof is never obtainable in matters of history. Each person who considers this historical question, however, must fair-mindedly assess the various explanatory options and select the one that fits the data best. Christians believe that God really did raise Jesus from the dead, and that this event is the once-for-all historical guarantee of the authenticity of Jesus's life work. Strange and unexpected as the resurrection was, it made sense of what Jesus said and did while he had been with them. It wasn't just some absurd event, a meaningless wonder, but, to them, a credible divine vindication.[9]

At least one more historical matter requires explanation, another fact that isn't miraculous in itself but points to some sort of extraordinary cause. As philosopher C. A. J. Coady says, "When an investigator decides to dismiss testimony to the unusual there is some onus upon him to explain how the false or misleading testimony came about."[10] Why have millions of people, across dozens of cultural lines—including highly trained historians and archaeologists and psychologists and psychiatrists around the world—come to believe the same doctrines as those first-century Jews, including this assertion of the resurrection of Jesus?[11] Can they *all* be simply credulous? *All* taking refuge in wish fulfillment? *All* setting aside their critical faculties for one wild, desperate hope?[12]

Of course, one must fairly ask the same question about any other religion or philosophy. But it wouldn't be, in fact, quite the same question. As we have seen, no other religion or philosophy makes *this kind* of claim. I can think of no other religion or philosophy that asks people to believe this strange an assertion about what actually happened in history.[13] So one last historical question about Christianity in particular remains interesting: Why have there been so many converts, of such different stripes, to such an apparently unbelievable story?

Could it be that people believe it only for the irreducible reason that it, somehow, is true?

Philosophical Grounds

According to Immanuel Kant, the fundamental questions any philosophy has to answer are these: "What can I know? What should I do? What may I hope?" (*Critique of Pure Reason*, 1781/1787). We might elaborate on Kant's formulation to say that the fundamental questions that any philosophy, any *functional* religion, has to answer are these—beyond the initial epistemological question, which we have already addressed: How well does this or that religion serve as the center of human life? How well does it explain the world and our place in it? How well does it recognize our highest good? How well does it diagnose what keeps us from that good? How well does it prescribe the solution to our problems? How well does it help us reach that highest good? A religion is an explanation of, and a response to, all of life—from one's most private inward experiences to the nature of the entire universe. So as we weigh up various religious options, we properly ask what religion best explains it all. What religion helps the most and in every way? What religion fits life?

These are the largest possible questions, requiring the largest possible answers. The brilliant Christian writer G. K. Chesterton (1874–1936) seemed never at a loss for words. Author of many books (including biographies, theology, thrillers, and his famous Father Brown mystery stories), editor of a weekly newspaper to which he was the major contributor, wide-ranging essayist, charming poet, and tireless gadfly, words flowed from Chesterton in an apparently unstoppable flood. In only one instance—this instance—did he admit that a question had (almost) dumbfounded him:

> It is very hard for a man to defend anything of which he is entirely convinced. It is comparatively easy when he is only partially convinced. He is partially convinced because he has found this or that proof of the thing, and he can expound it. But a man is not really convinced of a philosophic theory when he finds that something proves it. He is only really convinced when he finds that everything proves it. And the more converging reasons he finds pointing to this conviction, the more bewildered he is if asked suddenly to sum them up. Thus, if one asked an ordinary intelligent man, on the spur of the moment, "Why do you prefer civilization to savagery?" he would look wildly round at object after object, and would only be able to answer vaguely, "Why, there is that bookcase . . . and the coals in the coal-scuttle . . . and pianos . . . and policemen." The whole case for civilization is that the case for it is complex. It has done so many things. But that very multiplicity of proof which ought to make reply overwhelming makes reply impossible. . . . There is, therefore, about all complete conviction a kind of huge helplessness.[14]

Chesterton did recover his voice, of course, and went on to pen hundreds of pages over the rest of his life reflecting on various aspects of the world that did, to him, demonstrate the truth of the Christian religion. And this is the fundamental philosophical challenge: What picture of the world offered by what religion describes it all best—each particular (from bookcases to pianos, from the oxygen molecule to "Prélude à l'après-midi d'un faune," from child-rearing to taxation, and from surgery to football) and all together in a coherent whole?[15]

This challenge of comprehensive explanation—technically termed a *cumulative case* argument—is a point often overlooked both in polemics between devotees of various religions and by ordinary people just trying to sort things out. But we must not forget to keep things connected as we explore and evaluate. Religion A might well present an impressive view of one particular matter, but when one considers the wider implications, one is right to hesitate in embracing it. Take, for example, the teaching of Buddhism's Four Noble Truths about the suffering we incur in our doomed attachment to things that inevitably change—and finally disappear. Most of us have felt so awful at some point in our lives, and perhaps for extended seasons of our lives, that we have wondered whether, on balance, life is indeed best understood as *suffering*. We can't get everything we want, and we can't hold onto even to what we do get. In the end, and for many of us much sooner than later, weakness, suffering, and death take it all.

Buddhism's solution to this problem is to let go of it all, to find peace in detachment. You can't suffer if you don't care. But wouldn't you rather find a way to keep the good and shed the bad? Wouldn't you rather find a way to preserve the best of your life forever?

The Buddhist will smile and say, Well, of course. If we *could* have all the good and get rid of all the bad forever, who wouldn't want that? But the truth of the matter is that we cannot. So follow the Noble Eightfold Path and enjoy what relief there is available in nirvana.

Still, the Christian might then ask, isn't it odd that all over the world people manifest these aspirations to eternal life, to retain what is lovely, rather than, instead, to mildly enjoy things with detachment and then let them all go? Wouldn't it be sad—wouldn't it be in fact *disastrous*—if we forewent an actual path to eternal life and settled instead for detachment from life? Doesn't Christianity's promise of the splendid life to come square better with this universal aspiration than Buddhism's heroic renunciation?

Again, of course, our Buddhist friend might reply that humanity is in the grip of a deep delusion from which Buddhism alone can properly free us. And maybe that's true. All I'm suggesting here is that we owe it to ourselves to examine what grounds there are to subscribe to such a view of things when other apparently sensible people subscribe to an alternative that is much more in keeping with our aspirations.[16]

Consider also the New Atheists. They champion "selfish genes" and "survival of the fittest" as fundamental explanations for human behavior, but their views seem to founder on the facts of human life for which science cannot possibly give an adequate account. Diplomat Charles Malik provides a helpful list: "love, freedom, tragedy, decision, . . . loneliness, rebellion, suffering, resentment, ambition, hope, hopelessness"—and life and death themselves.[17]

Let's deal here with just two: altruism and beauty. According to the grim view of the world propagated by the New Atheists, there is really no such thing as genuine altruism, but only a sensible sort of selfishness. One looks after oneself, one's kin, one's community, and one's kind because the meaning of life is basically the reproduction of one's genes in one's progeny—or at least via one's relations. Yet why do at least some human beings insist on the goodness of caring for people who cannot possibly advantage the evolutionary imperative of passing along their genetic material to future generations? Why, in other words, do people insist on helping, sometimes self-sacrificially and even at the expense of their own actual spouses and children, those far away from themselves—geographically, culturally, economically, politically—who cannot possibly reciprocate?[18]

Why is there such a thing in the world as beauty that serves no evident evolutionary purpose? It's fine to say that this flower is colored and shaped in such a way as to maximize its reproductive potential. It attracts more bees by being so. But why do I, who cannot advantage this wildflower at all as I happen upon it during a walk in the woods, find it lovely? What is the evolutionary explanation for the drive motivating artists who strive to produce beauty even at the cost of their health, social status, and earning potential—all of which would normally be conducive to reproductive success?[19] Let's be clear: it is no discredit to science that it cannot fully explain beauty. As John Henry Newman once wrote, one can hardly blame science for being pressed into service to solve problems it has no instruments to solve.[20] Indeed, as theoretical physicist Freeman Dyson makes clear, science has its hands full in its own province:

> Wherever we go exploring in the world around us, we find mysteries. Our planet is covered by continents and oceans whose origin we cannot explain. Our atmosphere is constantly stirred by poorly understood disturbances we call weather and climate. The visible matter in the universe is outweighed by a much larger quantity of dark invisible matter that we do not understand at all. The origin of life is a total mystery, and so is the existence of human consciousness. We have no clear idea how the electrical discharges occurring in nerve cells in our brains are connected with our feelings and desires and actions.[21]

Science certainly cannot explain so very much *else* of life. As mathematician John Lennox puts it,

> Philosophy, literature, art, [and] music [lie] outside the scope of science strictly so-called. How can science tell us whether a poem is a bad poem or work of genius? Scarcely by measuring the

lengths of the words or the frequencies of the letters occurring in them. How can science possibly tell us whether a painting is a masterpiece or a confused smudge of colors? Certainly not by making a chemical analysis of the paint and the canvas. The teaching of morality likewise lies outside science. Science can tell you that, if you add strychnine to someone's drink, it will kill them. But science cannot tell you whether it is morally right or wrong to put strychnine into your grandmother's tea so that you can get your hands on her property.[22]

There is nothing "anti-science" in any of this. Christians, like anyone else, expect scientists—and especially "applied scientists" such as physicians and engineers—to work within the confines of the scientific method regardless of their religious views. A patient and her anxious family, even if they are fervent Christians, are going to seek another physician if the patient's surgeon says, "Yes, I suppose I could operate, but the Supreme Being is infinitely more capable of healing, so let's pray instead." The most pious of Christians don't want bridge-builders following what they recall God told them in a dream last night over what their load-bearing tests have shown them to be true.

It isn't that Christians don't *also* pray—for God to help the professionals do their work well and to enhance the effects of that work should God deign to do so, or even for a miracle if things look dire. It's that Christians believe that God normally works through *what normally works*. God doesn't intend human beings to be infants who merely squall for help to the heavenly Parent, but adults who grow in the capacity to live and work in the world God has made for us to enjoy and improve. Fulfilling our divinely given calling to cultivate the world entails that we normally attend to the world, try to understand it, and then interact with it as fruitfully as we can.

At the same time, we don't expect surgeons to write lyric poems about the patients on whom they have operated, nor engineers to decorate the bridges they build. Any given physician *might also* have a gift for poetry, but we recognize that it is a very different talent that is only slightly related to his medical skill. Science does what it does in many instances remarkably well. It just can't do everything, and it is silly, even irresponsible, to press it into unwilling service outside its domain.

For that matter, how ought we to understand science itself? Why does science arise in the medieval West, and not in the far older cultures of, say, China or India? Let's first be clear that science is not merely technology. Sociologist Rodney Stark makes the point that "a society does not have science simply because it can build sailing ships, smelt iron, or eat off porcelain dishes. . . . [The work of previous civilizations is better described as] lore, skills, wisdom, techniques, crafts, technologies, engineering, learning, or simply knowledge."[23] Science is a global intellectual enterprise of investigating the world in a disciplined reiteration of observation, hypothesis, and testing. It is a project, not merely a tool.

Science looks for regularities in nature—regularities that amount to predictable behavior—because science assumes there are such and it assumes that human minds are equipped to discover them and explain them. Christianity provides both the framework and the rationale for science. Christianity posits a God who creates a world and then sets over it a creature created to image God's own creativity in cultivating the world. To accomplish that great work of global care, we humans would have to be equipped with an orderly mind capable of generating reliable information about the world, and the world itself would have to be orderly, such that we could discern its regularities in order that we could then work with those regularities to comprehend and cultivate it.[24] Far from being the opponent of science, as some have asserted, Christianity both *grounds* and *motivates* science.[25]

This intrinsic relationship between science and Christianity versus the common tale of a putative "warfare" between them helps to explain a pertinent datum: the existence of scientists who are

Christians. Lots of them. Right back to the Scientific Revolution, in which all the major figures are, yes, Christians. (And their private papers indicate that, despite suggestions they simply mouthed Christian pieties in public to avoid scandal and persecution, those pioneers seem to have been generally quite devoted Christians.) It is suggestively ironic that while the New Atheists struggle to explain the fact of Christians somehow being also reputable scientists without apparent wrenching cognitive dissonance—even Dawkins concedes that he is acquainted with a few (!)—Christians have no trouble explaining atheistic scientists as those who are indebted, unaware, to the Christian worldview.[26]

Furthermore, as we have seen when we discussed the creation of the world in the Christian Story, Christianity provides an ethic to *guide* and *restrain* science—and its application in technology. There is abroad in the land the claim that Christianity's teaching that God set humanity over the rest of the world somehow gives the green light to human abuse of that world in rapacious agriculture, genetic manipulation, indifference to global climate change, and the rest of the list of sins against the planet. We would do far better, so this line of argument goes, if we would shed any spurious sense of our specialness and take our proper place as just one species among the others.[27]

That would be the very worst way for us to proceed, however. What other species cares about any other? Doesn't one species normally regard another only in terms of either threat or food? The Christian ethic provides the metaphysical and moral resources to restrain rapacity, to foster loving respect for our fellow creatures, and to take our place as the one species that is supposed to care for all the others.[28] Christianity can cast an appreciative but also a critical eye over technology. Not every new technique is good just because it is more efficient. Each innovation must be referred to the largest applicable scale of ethical considerations, with special attention to those most likely to be hurt, rather than advantaged, by new technologies. Christianity thus provides both impetus and discipline for science.[29] Besides Christianity's close relatives, Judaism and Islam, what other religion has—or does?[30]

Having set out all these arguments, however, I am suspicious when Christians claim to have philosophical *proofs* of their religion. Philosophical arguments that satisfy even a majority of philosophers as being even *likely* are notoriously hard to come by, let alone anything approaching a compelling demonstration.

My basic philosophical point is that in comparing philosophies/worldviews/religions we must admire where each is strong and also keep probing for what each does *not* explain well, or at all. If we then find that a particular religion explains certain things well but leaves badly under-explained or even glaringly unexplained aspects of experience that we hold nonetheless to be vitally important to life, we do well to hope that that religion isn't the best there is and to keep looking for something more satisfactory. At the end of the day, we might yet decide that this or that alternative is the best option on offer, even if it doesn't answer all our questions. But that conclusion should be reached only after a long and industrious day seeking diligently for a better solution.

To be sure, it seems that no matter what religion one opts for, mysteries will remain—as they do in any human attempt to understand reality. But it is one thing to say that we believers in Buddhism or the New Atheism haven't come up with a convincing answer yet to explain phenomenon X, even though we think we have very good arguments on other grounds to believe Buddhism or the New Atheism is true. It is quite another thing to provide a *bad* explanation for X, the explanation that is in fact *entailed by* the tenets of one's religion. That's a fatal kind of problem indeed, and it is a challenge I am leveling at Buddhism and the New Atheism—or, as it is more helpfully termed, "scientism."

It may also be the case that the teachings of a particular religion would lead one to *expect* certain mysteries about certain things while retaining faith in the general veracity of that religion. Christians have confidence in the Christian God and in the

Christian religion in the face of certain mysteries because we believe we have met Jesus, and that encounter provides what we need to know in order to trust in God, believe the Bible, and walk in step with the Church and the Holy Spirit. We acknowledge that there are important zones about which our knowledge is scanty. Given, nonetheless, what we believe about God, the world, and humanity, we are not surprised that we lack understanding about some things, including some very large matters—such as how the world came into existence, or how consciousness arose in the human animal, or how divine sovereignty and human freedom interact, or why some people convert to Christianity and others do not, or the meaning of this or that instance of dreadful suffering, and so on. From a Christian point of view, any philosophy that purported to neatly explain such matters would itself be deeply suspect as an oversimplified, merely human construct. Anything to do with God, as understood on Christian terms, is almost certainly to involve mystery to the human mind. On Christian premises certain matters *in their very nature* can be expected to remain beyond our ken. We trust in the truth of the gospel on grounds that do fall within the light of our limited capacities.

This is a delicate matter, and I want to be very clear about what I am asserting and what I am not. I am not saying that Christians can retreat into the convenient category of "mystery" whenever an interlocutor challenges the quality of our thinking. I am saying that some matters can be expected to remain at least somewhat mysterious, given a Christian view of things. The challenger quite rightly can then expect the Christian to give an account of the world so well grounded in what *can* be rationally assessed as to justify suspending judgment in these other areas. Not just any subject or assertion can be roped off as "mystery," safely immune to critical examination. But some zones can be seen to be mysterious in a way that is rationally coherent with the Christian worldview.

The fair-minded inquirer will grant all of this, especially when our top scientists tell us that, between dark matter and dark energy, we really don't know much about 90 percent of the universe. Perhaps we do know enough about the cosmos, however, to rule out some beliefs as simply unbelievable. What about miracles? Since Christianity has a whopper of a miracle right at its center— the resurrection of Jesus—perhaps it can be set aside as a serious religious option because it is literally incredible.

David Hume, the great skeptic, certainly thought so, and many have repeated some version of Hume's argument in the several centuries since he set it out.[31] In essence, according to Hume, miracle stories ought not to be believed because they are so fundamentally at odds with everything else we know. However persuasive the account might be, however trustworthy the testimony might appear, the suggestion that a miracle occurred has to be weighed against the heavy fact that we ourselves have never witnessed a miracle. In addition, no one we know well and trust thoroughly has ever witnessed one. Moreover, we know that putative accounts of miracles have repeatedly been exposed as fraudulent or, at best, overblown products of mass hysteria at revival meetings and the like. Yes, people claim to have had a too-short leg grow a bit, or a pain recede somewhat, or even a cancer go into remission for a while. But show me an amputee whose limb grew back. Show me a missing organ—an eye or a kidney—that suddenly appeared. Show me, best of all, a truly, unmistakably dead person who—after hours and hours of no-doubt-about-it death, not a few seconds or a few minutes of "clinical death"—comes back to life. Not only are such cases not readily available, they aren't reported at all by anyone whom any of us take seriously.

Hume's technical argument deserves a technical response in technical literature, and it certainly has received that over the intervening years.[32] But we can be fair to Hume, I think, by saying two complementary things. On his own grounds, he seems right. On other grounds, he doesn't. To put it more provocatively, Hume's argument against believing in miracles is either probably correct or wildly wrong.

Given Hume's situation—in the Scottish Enlightenment of the eighteenth century—it's no wonder he doubted miracle stories. We can take at face value his declaration that he had never seen a miracle, nor had anyone he knew seen one. The world was an orderly place. The whole agenda of the Enlightenment, in fact, was to understand the world as such, in the spirit of the Scientific Revolution: to discover the regularities, even the laws, by which everything existed, the way Newton & Co. had formulated laws of physics. Not only everything in Hume's experience, but everything he *wanted* to constitute his experience, pointed away from divine interventions and toward the orderliness of things. The historical evidence that God raised Jesus from the dead could never outweigh the cumulative experience of Hume's entire life and the collective experience of everyone in his culture. Miracles empirically don't occur in Hume's world, so they don't occur anywhere. Indeed, nothing in that world is more sure than that dead is dead. Some other explanation for Jesus's empty tomb, his enthusiastic disciples, and all the rest of it simply must be better than that the Supreme Being decided to reach down into the world and re-animate a corpse. The Supreme Being manifestly doesn't do such things, so He didn't.

The story of Jesus's resurrection, however, takes place in a different context from eighteenth-century Edinburgh. Jesus's life, death, and putative coming-back-to-life take place in a Jerusalem informed by centuries of Yhwh's governing of his people. During those centuries Yhwh has performed many interventionist wonders, starting with the Exodus itself. Remember all those plagues, then the parting of the Red Sea, and then the drowning of Pharaoh and his army? Jews did. They reminded each other of those miracles every Passover, and still do.

Jesus himself had performed miracles over and over again in the presence of his disciples. In fact, the Bible doesn't refer to them as "miracles," which could be understood as simply "shocking events that seem to go beyond what we expect of nature," but as "signs" (John 2:11, 3:2)—parables in action, object lessons in divine power, yes, but also of divine intention, each one signifying the kind of God Yhwh is and the kind of work Jesus is doing in God's name. Jesus doesn't perform parlor tricks of trivial surprise and amusement. He always, always does something *significant*, something that illustrates the Great Narrative of God's generous and saving dealings with Israel and the world: healing diseases or injuries, exorcising demons, stilling storms, feeding hungry followers, even raising the dead.

In such a context—the context of the whole Old Testament of God's mighty acts and of Jesus's several years of sign-studded ministry as well—the idea that God raises Jesus from the dead to vindicate him and his teaching not only seems un-arbitrary, but, now that one thinks about it, actually predictable. (Jesus did predict it, of course, and even suggested that Old Testament prophets had glimpsed something of it, too.) The resurrection of Jesus is, in retrospect and in context, just what one would expect to happen— even though no one but Jesus seems to have expected it. Far from defying everything we think we know about how the world works, per Hume, the resurrection of Jesus fits nicely with everything the Jews knew about how God works, and how God had just been working, scant days before, in the public ministry of Jesus himself.

So hermeneutics reappears in our conversation. What one finds plausible, let alone credible, depends very much on one's social location and personal experience. It is understandable that David Hume found miracles in general, and this one in particular, so incongruous with the world as he understood it that he felt he simply had to rule them out. Perhaps they had happened, he would allow, but there was no way he could rationally justify believing that they did.

In a different situation, however, one might find the resurrection of Jesus not just believable, but entirely appropriate.[33] *Of course* God wouldn't leave Jesus to rot in a tomb, disgraced and discouraging to his disciples who were on the verge of abandoning his cause and returning to their former lives (John 21:3). *Of course* God would show who was who and what was what by raising Jesus from the dead in such a way both that his disciples could be encouraged and that his enemies would be unable to gainsay the event—and yet without overwhelming everyone with evidence that would compel assent of those who were yet unwilling to repent.

God is not interested in merely impressing humans with the divine presence and power. (The Bible actually makes this point in terms of Satan and his minions being well acquainted with those facts while their resistance remains firm [James 2:19].) God is focused instead on what centrally matters: our salvation from the inside out. So God allows ambiguity in the evidence in order to give room for resistant doubt. After all, we don't know everything that happened during those weeks surrounding Jesus's trial, death, and purported resurrection. Who knows what we might yet discover that could radically change the picture? Maybe that body disappeared through some natural course of events, and likewise maybe those disciples suddenly became gloriously confident proclaimers of the resurrection of their Master because of, well, delusion, or deception, or something. So perhaps not much ambiguity after all—at least not in terms of the evidence we *do* have, which are the grounds on which most sensible people attempt to make decisions, rather than holding out indefinitely for what may or may not emerge. When you see it from the Christian point of view in the context of the early believers, you might well conclude that Christians possess very strong grounds after all to believe that God the Father did raise Jesus from the dead, thus vindicating him and his work, and thus validating the Christian message as The Good News for the whole world.

History and philosophy thus come together in the Christian worldview to provide what Christians, at least, see to be compelling reasons to believe. But Christianity is, after all, far more than a description of what happened in the career of Jesus. His career was not a wonder meant to impress upon us the fact of God's existence, or of his divine nature, or any other abstract proposition. Christianity is about life well lived. So what are the ethical and pragmatic grounds on which Christians find Christianity believable?

Ethical and Pragmatic Grounds

Let's begin with the most basic question: Why be moral? Why try to be good—why strive to develop and then be true to a moral system, an understanding of right and wrong that transcends mere instinct and impulse?

Some have tried to formulate ethics on the basis of a pleasure/pain calculus: act in these ways and maximize pleasure, avoid those ways and minimize pain. But how is this moral rather than merely shrewd?[34]

Why do anything that is not to one's advantage? Altruism seems to be at the heart of our moral intuitions; it seems *good* to sacrifice one's own interests for the welfare of others. But is that inclination, as social Darwinists as well as many others would suggest, merely a function of the evolutionary drive to propagate oneself—perhaps overextended to those who cannot, in fact, assist us in any way in that quest?

Why be good when no one is watching? Why uphold an ethical standard—whatever it is, however one came by it—simply on the grounds that one *ought* to do it, that some actions or agendas are inherently good and others are inherently bad, even if honoring them comes at a cost? Perhaps one trains oneself in conventional morality so as to please oneself and attract the attention of a mate of similar conviction—but is that morality, or just self-interest translated into moral language?

I was once enjoying a fine supper on a cruise ship. At our table were seated several other couples we had just met. The conversation took a serious turn once it was discovered what I did for a living. The two couples nearest me, one pair from France and the other from England, made it very clear that they were atheists. They all averred with some vehemence that they didn't need God or to believe in God to be good. Moreover, they knew lots of other atheists who were far more admirable in generosity and integrity and loyalty than were many Christians in their acquaintance. What did I think of *that*?

I could not but agree, since my field of acquaintance is peopled by similar folk. What I said in response was this: "I am sure that's true, and I am just very glad that you all are Christian atheists."

They stared back at me. I continued, "I have traveled to other parts of the world that have been dominated by forms of religion and philosophy that vary quite a lot from the heritage of the West: China, for instance. Those people are atheists, too, but they hold some very different values than you and I happen to hold in common. And you and I hold those values in common because of that Western heritage, which was largely shaped by Christianity. So, as I say, I'm very glad you're *Christian* atheists, since we can agree ethically on quite a lot, versus, say, a Maoist atheist or a wealth-chasing atheist."

Of course atheists can be good without God. Many of them clearly are. But can any of them be *coherently* good without God? They believe that the cosmos is constituted merely by matter and energy in motion, in which life emerges in a happy chance and consciousness likewise, so that morality is—well, what? A strategy for reproductive success (Wilson)? A social contract to lessen violence and promote security (Hobbes)? A mere legitimation of power (Marx)? A rationally derived code to maximize the good life and minimize threats to it—begging the question of who decides what "good" means (Mill)? And do any of these options amount to what we all mean by *morality*, a binding sense of *ought,* rather than reducing to mere techniques for rearranging what *is*—according to the deciders' own sense of optimal living? Even those atheists who affirm a transcendent moral order in the cosmos cannot do more than *affirm* it. They have no reliable way of determining what that moral order actually is beyond their own intuitions, no compelling way of adjudicating between dissimilar intuitive moral codes. In short, I suggest that my atheist supper companions are so commendably moral not because they are atheists but because they are (put more carefully) *post-Christian* atheists whose values are actually rooted in the moral norms of Christianity—versus, say, the moral norms of Stoicism, Daoism, or Maoism.[35]

Christianity tells a Story that makes moral sense of the world. The Story is framed, as all stories are, by a moral framework that implies a set of ethical values. Those values, Christians believe, constitute a coherent system that affirms many generic moral intuitions (even as it sometimes corrects them) and gives good grounds for their validity. Let's take up altruism again, since it is perhaps the purest form of ethical action, and let's see how Christianity confirms our regard for it while also, perhaps, correcting our understanding of it.

Why care for others, especially those who cannot care for you in return, or in any other way advantage you? The great Christian leader Martin Luther posed a powerful answer to that question half a millennium ago. He wrote that God in Christ has done for us what we cannot possibly do for ourselves, providing us riches beyond imagination in this world and in the world to come. Already in this life, God has given us forgiveness of sins, reconciliation with God and each other, and the power to live better lives. Beyond death, furthermore, God promises us an infinitely extended future of health, security, delight, and value.

We could not possibly be good enough to deserve such rewards, Luther said: they are gifts of a generous God. All we have to do is accept them from God's hand and live according to the new relationship God has established with us, variously understood, as we have seen, in the Biblical pictures of a new family, a new marriage, a new employment, and so on. We now do what God wants us to do not out of the hope of profiting ourselves, but out of gratitude and love for what God has done, is doing, and will do for us. Christianity avoids qualifying altruism, as is seen in some other religions: "Do this selfless thing—or else you'll suffer!" One never can forget one's own interests, but is always caring for others out of an agenda to better one's lot in this world and whatever world is to come. Genuine altruism is possible only when one's (legitimate) interest in one's own welfare is abundantly looked after by God's generosity. Then one is truly free to care for others without regard to personal gain.[36]

Still, isn't there something valid in the sense that by helping others I am yet helping myself?

At least since the Swedish theologian Anders Nygren championed the idea of *agapē* as the highest form of love and defined it as utter selflessness, caring for others without the slightest regard for oneself, Christians have been telling each other that this is fundamentally how God loves and how God expects us to love as well.[37] But is this understanding of love psychologically possible, or even conceptually coherent?

Let me introduce you to my useless grandson, Jude. At the time of this writing, Jude is just two years old. He's cute, yes, but he's also very demanding. Feeding, watering, cleaning, diapering, amusing, soothing, protecting, guiding—the kid is exhausting. And for what? He doesn't pay for his care. He doesn't look after anyone else. He doesn't even thank his caregivers, but soaks it all up like a sponge and expects it all to continue.

And it will continue, of course, because I love Jude, and so do his fine parents, and so do his other grandparents, and so do a host of other relations and friends. The child is surrounded by people who are in fact eager to give to him without any expectation of recompense.

Or is that quite right? Look at how hard we all work at getting Jude's attention and particularly at getting him to smile, let alone laugh. Look at how much time and money we spend buying clothes and foods and toys we hope Jude will enjoy, going well beyond what he needs to survive. His happiness, not just his basic existence, means a lot to us. Now here's the point. Because we love him, we promote his happiness. And here's the paradox. Because we love him, his happiness promotes our happiness. So our altruism is truly selfless in the sense that Jude cannot possibly return it *in kind*, or, really, do very much of anything with intentionality at this stage of his life. (Later, he'll be able to draw pictures that will decorate our refrigerator doors, but unless he's a prodigy they won't go far to justify all the expense we will have gone to by that stage.) No, it's a one-way street—except that it's actually a circle.

Love is a circle of mutual implication. It's what I call the "win-win-win scenario."[38] God commands us to love God, each other, and the world. If we do, however, we find that we benefit also from playing our roles in that economy of mutual care because the world has been created such that our welfare is bound up in the welfare of others. It's not just the symbiosis of participating in an ecology of mutual dependence. It's the interleaving of *love*, the connecting of my well-being with yours, and of yours with mine, and of ours with theirs through love, through positive relationship. At his age, Jude cannot pay me back for services rendered. At thirty he might be able to—but how grotesque it would be if I then presented him with an invoice with a request for remuneration. It doesn't cross a normal person's mind to do such a thing because we love each other, and thus promoting the other's welfare promotes our own joy as well.

God loves like this, for this is the meaning of love, of voluntarily binding one's heart to the other's flourishing. The New Testament Epistle to the Hebrews encourages Christians to follow Jesus's example: "Let us run with perseverance the race that is set before us, looking to Jesus, the pioneer and perfecter of our faith, who *for the sake of the joy that was set before him* endured the cross, disregarding its shame, and has taken his seat at the right hand of the throne of God" (12:1–2; emphasis added). The Gospel according to John says this: "God so loved the world that he gave his only Son, so that everyone who believes in him may not perish but may have eternal life" (3:16). Father and Son loved us enough to consent to the Cross—by which their own happiness would be secured *because ours would be, and love wants that.* Around and around the circle of love goes the benefit of good actions, not stopping at any one place at the cost of another. I gladly care for my grandson, as I care for my grown sons, at considerable cost to myself, because when they thrive, I thrive, and when they suffer, I suffer. I don't have to try to prefer their welfare to mine in some heroic act of selflessness. I simply love them and I therefore *want* to help them, and when they are helped, I benefit, too.

So far, so good, in the context of a mutually affectionate family. But God's command is for us to love our neighbors whether we like them or not. Jesus commanded us to love our *enemies*. What is "love" in that mode?

Love is caring for the other, considering the other's interests and then actively seeking them to the extent that one can. It isn't sentiment, but determined action. And that we can do toward anyone, like them or not—although needing assistance from God, to be sure, in truly seeking the welfare of our enemies. Thus Christians have gone around the world founding orphanages and hospitals, schools and universities, publishing houses and broadcast stations, farms and factories—regardless of whether the people they were helping were Christians or even likely to become Christians. No other religion has that record. Not one.[39] No other religion has even attempted it, because no other religion commands it or provides adequate grounds even to commend it—even religions, such as the Mahayana tradition of Buddhism, that highly value the virtue of compassion. Christianity's imperative to *love* one's neighbor in every dimension of that neighbor's need, from spiritual to financial, is unique.[40] As the scholar of West African religion Lamin Sanneh put it, "Solidarity with the poor, the weak, the disabled, and the stigmatized is the sine qua non of Christianity's credibility as a world religion"—much, we might say, to the consternation of Nietzsche and his ilk.[41]

For millions of people across cultures and centuries, following the Christian way feels right, sound, healthy, moral, affirmative of good, and opposed to evil. True, throughout history there have been people who, in the name of the Christian religion or while occupying a clerical office, have committed sins, some of them heinous. The usual suspects, Crusaders and Inquisitors, need to be acknowledged immediately, but also so many preachers, priests, politicians, and parents—the list of villains can be long indeed.[42]

Note, however, that such people are condemned by the very faith they purport to serve. The Christian religion forbids the torture and slaughter of other people simply because they do not believe as we do. Authentic Christianity, as evidenced in the life of its Founder and the documents constituting its Scripture, never condones abuse, never advocates subjugation and exploitation. Many Christian *people*, alas, have been as evil as anyone else, and often they have tried to justify their evil from the Bible itself. But they stand under the verdict of their own religion and will one day lower their eyes under the steady gaze of their ostensible Lord, Jesus Christ. For who would plausibly identify Jesus of Nazareth with these horrors? Who would convincingly trace these evils back to his teaching and example?[43]

In our time, dark troubles persist. Evil—both in directed malevolence and in confused stupidity and pride—still bedevils the Christian church. The serious inquirer does well to look past the depressing failures, however, and consider the faith as set out in its guiding documents and as manifest in those who practice the faith most consistently, and judge it from there. This is what one ought to do if one is looking into Zen Buddhism, or Aboriginal traditions, or Marxism. One should look at the best exemplars of the religion or philosophy in question, not those who manifestly fail to practice it properly.[44]

The basic claim of Christian morality is that it defines the world accurately and prescribes the best way to live in it. Christian principles are not arbitrary or even just symbolic—mere cultural markers to set off the Christian tribe, so to speak, from others. Christianity claims that the God who made us all has given us a kind of owner's manual in the Bible: a guide not only to God's preferences but to the very grain of the universe. God loves us and wants us to thrive in that universe, so God has taught us what we need to know. Christianity therefore once again subjects itself to scrutiny. Does living in the way it prescribes in fact lead to flourishing?

The evidence is at least suggestive. Consider the typical markers of mental and social well-being: stability and satisfaction in marriage, willingness to volunteer and contribute financially to charity (and not just religious institutions), engagement in the community (from sports to politics), sexual happiness, even longevity itself. Observant Christians—not just people who claim to be Christians, but people who actually go to church regularly, read the Bible and pray regularly, teach their children the faith, and so on—score remarkably higher on such metrics than the population at large.[45] As sociologist Kurt Bowen observes, if everyone were to behave like these people, charitable giving, volunteering, and a number of other social goods would go up—a lot. In a remarkably pointed conclusion to almost three hundred pages of carefully modulated sociological analysis, Bowen writes,

> If the expanding body of the Non Religious [sic] is our guide to the future, we may reasonably expect that life satisfaction will decline, concern for others will diminish, marriage will grow more fragile, family and friendship networks will shrink, volunteering will become less frequent, and we will grow ever less generous in our so very affluent world. In a word, our civility is threatened. If this is the victory that secularism and the Enlightenment have wrought, then we have no cause to celebrate.[46]

We dare not whitewash reality. Religious people can be awful, and in many various ways. We have all seen that churches and families and even communities of very intense religious commitment can shelter abusers—from pompous and exploitative pastors to sexually transgressive relatives.[47] Some religious people insist on transmuting the glowing gold of conscientious morality into the lifeless lead of legalism—feeling driven to achieve perfect little lives while condemning everyone around them who doesn't similarly strive. And being well-churched doesn't always translate into a comprehensive Christian ethic, if churches confine their teaching to the narrow zones of personal piety and evangelistic endeavor. (For two very different examples, think of Rwandans massacring each other in the 1990s, despite being the most churched nation in Africa, and of Sioux County, Iowa, which, despite very high church attendance, in the 2010s strongly supported and repeatedly elected Rep. Steve King, an openly racist congressman.) The New Testament itself is full of examples of, and warnings about, truly wicked people within Christian ranks—even whole churches going astray. Merely hoisting the Christian flag doesn't change what's going on underneath it.

It isn't news that people can be bad, even—and sometimes especially—when they wrap themselves in religious robes. What seems, alas, to be news is when people are remarkably good, and the record shows that serious Christians generally have something going on that is worth a serious look. Christianity promises power for continual upward spiritual development. The universal testimony of Christians is that they do receive help toward personal maturity: through the moral guidance of the Church, through the inspiration and instruction of the Bible, through the transforming experience of prayer, through the moral strength of the Holy Spirit within them, and so on. People acquainted with Christian converts have often remarked as well on the life-changing and life-improving effects of their embracing Christianity. So not only in its teachings, but also in the experience of practicing those teachings, Christianity offers moral power.

Readers who know professing Christians whose lives seem less than admirable will balk at this claim. "They're no different than I am," one might assert, "and some of them are worse!" In response to this sensible objection, we may make three observations.

First, Christianity does not claim to make new converts instantly perfect, only progressively better. God reaches individuals at a particular point in their lives, rescues them from spiritual death, and sets them on the path to purity and health. (Not everyone has an exciting experience of conversion, to be sure. Many Christians grow up in the faith and experience it as a progressive deepening of commitment.) Some people are greater sinners than others and come to faith later in life, so as relatively new converts with terrible pasts and destructive habits they will compare poorly with some other people—in absolute moral terms. Relative to where they were before, however, they yet may be manifesting gratifying progress.

Second, Christianity is about God working with human beings, not puppets or robots. Christians continue to have a will that can resist God, retard development, and retain bad habits of sin. It is not necessarily the fault of the Christian faith that Christians act badly, for it is we Christians ourselves who act badly. A music teacher can hardly be blamed for a student's poor performance if the student fails to practice and heed instruction. A parent cannot be blamed for a child's misbehavior if the parent has (by some objective standard) raised the child well and yet the child chooses his or her own way. God does not turn Christians into automatons, but cooperates with us as we will allow—much, no doubt, to God's frustration and disappointment, yet as part of the divine plan to develop spiritually mature human beings.

Third, cultural dynamics continue to encourage some people to claim adherence to the Christian religion when they in fact do not adhere to it in any meaningful way. There are areas in Canada and the United States in which it is still economically and socially advantageous to attend church, mouth Christian platitudes, profess Christian identity, and in other respects act superficially as believers. For larger parts of both populations, there is a residual memory of Christianity received from family, school, and regional or national culture. Thus people continue to tell pollsters that they are Christians although they never attend church, do not read the

Bible, rarely pray, and know virtually nothing about Christian doctrine and history. Let us recognize that someone who never worshipped in a mosque, neglected the Qur'an, ignored the daily prayers, and knew nothing of the shari'ah (the path of obedience) could freely call himself a Muslim, but no informed person would take his claim seriously. It is important not to assess Christianity's claim to spiritual transformation by the example of nominal adherents, but rather by the lives of faithful practitioners.[48]

Christianity does not claim to effect transformation on the individual level alone. It also claims to integrate people into communities of holiness and love. Indeed, Jesus's own command to his first followers was to obey his teachings and love each other so deeply and well that others would remark on this mutual affection and service as the very sign of Christian community (John 13:33–34). As ethicist John Howard Yoder puts it,

> The church can be a foretaste of the peace for which the world was made. . . . Transcendence is kept alive . . . by the vitality of communities in which a different way of being keeps breaking in here and now. That we can really be led on a different way is the real proof of the transcendent power which offers hope of peace to the world as well.[49]

If Christian churches are manifestly not communities of exemplary goodness, then Christianity is failing to deliver on its promise.

No one can deny that Christian churches frequently do fail. Isn't it painfully obvious that some churches are just groups of self-centered, self-promoting individuals, no different from a so-cial club or political party—except perhaps lacking in the graces of the former and the usefulness of the latter? Still, many people who have been in crisis would say that their churches are succeeding. Churches—ordinary, neighborhood churches—have rallied wonderfully around the sick, the poor, the lonely, the discouraged, the overwhelmed. Many people have converted to the Christian faith precisely because of the love they have witnessed among local Christians, as well as because of kindness they have received from such Christians. These stories do not make headlines, of course, but they are not the less authentic and important for that.

Many Christian churches manifestly fail this test of exemplary love, but explanations for such failure aren't hard to find. Churches, like individuals, are communities in process. In such churches struggling to be and do better, those of us who don't feel perfect ourselves can feel accepted. Moreover, churches, like individuals, sometimes do, but sometimes do not, cooperate with the leadership of the Holy Spirit. And, obviously, not every organization that calls itself a Christian church is, in any important sense of the term, truly Christian.

None of these considerations exonerate Christians who fail to live up to their Master's demands. But the fair-minded person should hold these Christians only to the standards of their own faith, not to some impossible perfection, even as it is also right to expect Christians to strive for ever-greater fidelity.

What, then, is the actual case? Do Christians in general, in fact, love each other—again, in the practical Biblical sense of caring for each other, not in the sentimental sense of harboring warm feelings for each other? The answer to this question is best sought on two levels: the macroscopic (all of the churches) and microscopic (this particular church). This is not, however, how many people con-sider the question. Critics pull together a few anecdotes and a news clipping or two, this personal bad experience and that rumor, an atrocity story from history and a recent outrage from the internet, and from this arbitrary mélange purport to arrive at a valid conclu-sion about an entire world religion.

We would all do better to consider the macro level, of the cur-rent worldwide state and the previous two-thousand-year history of the Christian religion, as we have done along the way in this book. Then we would be entitled to make general conclusions. On the micro level, we ought to enter the doors of an authentic

Christian fellowship and examine the society we find. It takes time to understand the dynamics of such a group—as it takes time for a good anthropologist to study any culture, and particularly if the anthropologist is careful not to let prejudices get in the way of disciplined analysis. In sum, surveying the history of the Christian church as a whole and closely observing a living community of sincere Christians surely offers much more to the serious inquirer than a superficial survey of this or that set of disappointments and scandals.

There are other things Christianity is supposed to accomplish in the world. Christians are supposed to make converts, and clearly the world's largest religion has succeeded, however dubious and temporary some of those conversions have been. Christians are supposed to work with God toward shalom. Sometimes we have, dedicating ourselves to political, economic, cultural, or racial justice. But it is personal transformation and the building of loving community that constitute the heart of the Christian promise. And on this score, while disappointments must be acknowledged, millions of Christians around the world testify that Christianity truly works.

What, then, about that other great challenge to the scientism of our time—and, frankly, to Buddhism and a wide range of other options competing for our attention and allegiance—namely, beauty? Do the grounds for commending Christianity extend to the aesthetic?

Aesthetic Grounds

In the initial outline for this book, I intended at this juncture to write about the beauty prompted by Christianity: all those artists over all those centuries, from Fra Angelico to J. S. Bach to T. S. Eliot, who were inspired by the heroes of the faith, by the powerful narratives and symbols in the Bible and Christian tradition, and above all by the magnetic and mysterious figure of Jesus. But Christianity doesn't always emphasize beauty the way some other religions do. Sikh gurdwaras typically are awash in gilt and color; only some Christian churches dazzle, while many are austere, some are just plain, and more than a few are ugly. The gorgeous Lord Krishna of devotional Hinduism radiates bluely from every gold-rimmed portrait and porcelain statue of him, while Jesus is literally nondescript in the Bible, physically so unremarkable that when it came time to arrest him, Judas Iscariot had to greet Jesus with a kiss to distinguish him from his disciples. Moreover, that Bible itself is hardly a paragon of high style in ancient literature. Brilliant as it is in many passages, it also manifests the various authors' idiosyncrasies and even difficulties in Hebrew or Greek. How different is this scripture when compared with the orthodox Islamic claim that the Qur'an is written in luminously perfect Arabic, the very speech of God?

Is there a distinctive Christian aesthetic? Hardly. Christian art has been generated over twenty centuries and in hundreds of cultures, so Christian art is as variegated as are the world's various artistic traditions. While the Christian Story provides a repertoire of topics and themes and tropes to inspire the world's artists and artistic traditions, Christianity does not itself generate a characteristic way of producing art. (In fact, the only Christian artistic rule is a negative one, inherited from ancient Israel: avoid making idols.)[50]

What, then, does Christianity have to commend itself to those concerned with the aesthetic dimension of life? Quite a lot, actually.

First, Christianity takes intuition and imagination seriously as essential elements in our general comprehension of things.[51] The Bible itself is a compendium of a wide range of literary genres, only a few of which appeal straightforwardly to discursive reasoning. Most of the Bible appeals instead to intuition and the imagination: narrative, both historical and fictive; prophecy, typically couched in visions, allusions, and metaphors; and poetry cropping up everywhere—even an entire book of love songs. Jesus himself is constantly telling stories, offering illustrations, composing similes, and referring to himself in metaphors: door, shepherd, housewife, vine, hen, and many more. The Bible is constantly encouraging us to lift our heads and *see*—"Behold!" is one of its favorite commands.

Precisely because the Bible's subject matter (God, the world, and everything, both evil and good) exceeds our descriptive abilities in science and philosophy, and because the Bible is intended to instruct, inform, and inspire people of every age and profession and culture, the Bible abundantly employs art and appeals to artistic apprehension—which does not exclude rational reflection, of course, but certainly transcends it. The artistic imagination is thus integral to the Christian way of experiencing, comprehending, and living in the world.

Second, Christianity offers justification for the beautiful. The Creator creates creatures to be creative—that's the story of human origins in Genesis 1. God manifestly loves creating—as psalm after psalm makes plain. How many species of beetles does the global ecosystem actually need? Why isn't three hundred thousand enough? Think of all the beauty with which God has decorated the world that only God has been able to appreciate. God has adorned the cosmos with far more beauty than any utilitarian purpose would require— from deserts at sunset to gigantic nebulae in distant reaches of the cosmos to whirling symmetries at the subatomic level. Christianity can explain the presence of this beauty and of our apprehension of it as such, yes, and also validate the quest for beauty, our hunger for it, as a good—indeed, as a godly—thing. (I am not ignoring the problem of evil, including evil in the natural world, which we will engage later. For now, I'm looking at the good things in nature, which *also* require explanation.)

God blesses beauty for its own sake. Vermeer's *Girl with a Pearl Earring* does not have to *do* anything but just *be* lovely. To be sure, Christianity warns against self-indulgence in art, architecture, and personal adornment (Hosea 8:14; 1 Timothy 2:9)—the conspicuous consumption that can seduce the rich and even the marginally well-off alike. And, *pace* Keats, the Bible cautions also against equating beauty with goodness or truth. Israel was warned frequently about confusing beauty with virtue in selecting kings, and the Proverbs are replete with warnings of evil seducing the unwary in a beautiful disguise. A number of Biblical characters (Saul, Absalom, Delilah, Salome) are portrayed as impressively attractive and yet foolish— or worse. Indeed, some Christians have been so impressed with the Bible's cautions in these respects as to go to the opposite ascetic extreme of commending plainness, even ugliness, as intrinsically virtuous. But physical beauty is not scorned in the Bible either. Heroes such as Joseph, David, Esther, and Daniel and his three friends are all described as comely. And the New Jerusalem itself is described in terms of glittering extravagance.[52]

Christianity also offers aesthetic justification for a variety of important modes of art beyond the conventionally lovely. Christianity sings adoring hymns to a crucified man (as in Isaac Watts's classic "When I Survey the Wondrous Cross") and paints word pictures in its Scriptures of profound themes well beyond the beautiful (from Ecclesiastes's Weltschmerz to Ezekiel's bizarre street performances and vivid visions). Christianity endorses the legitimate power of the sublime, whether the subject matter is explicitly religious or not: from Matthias Grünewald's Isenheim Altarpiece to Pablo Picasso's *Guernica*. It validates the provocative: from Hieronymus Bosch's dreamscapes to Francis Bacon's *Three Studies for Figures at the Base of a Crucifixion*. And it even welcomes the transgressive: from Michelangelo's Sistine Chapel nudes to the formaldehyde-preserved animals and diamond-encrusted skulls of Damien Hirst. Furthermore, Christianity does not simply applaud everything that might want to go under the name of art, since it condemns all selfishness, from the brutal to the trivially self-indulgent.

Third, Christianity can explain whence creativity arises. In his massive study of creative people, psychologist Mihaly Csikszentmihalyi records testimony after testimony describing the creative moment as a *gift*. Composers, activists, architects, engineers, executives—all of them are learned, all of them are brilliant, all of them are highly motivated, but none of them believe they know how to produce or discover a truly creative idea. Instead, the vector is reversed: the idea comes to them. Some ascribe the gift-giving to God; those without faith in a deity report the experience nonetheless as a kind of *reception*.[53] Christians are pretty sure we know how to account for that mysterious, but widely acknowledged, experience. The God who reveals himself in the first chapter of the Bible as creative created us creatures to be creative—and loves to help us be so.

Likewise, Christians have an answer to the question of why the cosmos somehow ends up producing a da Vinci, a Shakespeare, or a Beethoven. It's hard to see the evolutionary advantage to the race of such artistic gifts, or to being oneself aesthetically gifted—stereotypes of glamorous artists seducing a string of admirers notwithstanding. Law professor Steven Smith writes about

> a former colleague who by his own account was incapable of religious faith but was deeply sensitive to art and music, and who confided in me that he was troubled by a naturalistic worldview because he could find no real home in it (as opposed to unsatisfying, tone-deaf evolutionary *explanations*) for Mozart's lofty compositions. The sublimity of the "Jupiter" symphony or the *Requiem* [is] undeniably real. So if evolutionary naturalism cannot adequately account for this sublimity, then . . . well, my colleague honestly wasn't sure what conclusion to draw.[54]

It's not difficult, however, to see from a Christian point of view why a creative Creator blesses the world with creatives.

Finally, Christianity offers moral justification for the production and enjoyment of art even as it raises those very questions. In a world of stark basic needs, in which millions starve and groan under oppression, many of us ask how one can justify buying paints and brushes and spending hours rendering a still life. How can we justify enjoying such a work on a wall, whether our own or a gallery's? Christianity does not call artists to abandon their studios to serve in soup kitchens or refugee centers, although some artists might well want to engage in both forms of service. It calls each person to use his or her gifts to bless the world as richly as each of us can. From a Christian viewpoint, the world has been supplied by God with enough to go around. The problem is not a lack of resources, such that we must rob Peter (art) to pay Paul (charity). It is we human beings who interrupt its proper distribution and we human beings who must solve those political and military and ideological problems through people with the apposite abilities to confront such challenges effectively—that is, through political engagement and military intervention and ideological contest— rather than compelling skilled artists to become clumsy social workers or inept activists. Put differently, the fact that some people are not yet succeeding in their callings to provide food and justice and security for the world does not entail artists neglecting their distinctive calling.[55]

Art does not need justification on some other grounds. Yes, art can indeed make the workplace more exciting, thus prompting higher productivity. It can make the advertisement more compelling, thus prompting higher sales. It can make the spokesperson more alluring, thus prompting higher concurrence. Art can do all those things, and in some cases it should, although of course in other cases it shouldn't.[56] But art is like sport, and romance, and play, and comedy: not strictly necessary, in terms of basic physical survival, but truly essential to human life. That's why all four of these show up even in concentration camps. Not all religions can make sense of that reality and endorse those priorities, but Christianity can, and does.

Still, at its heart the Christian religion does not place art, or even beauty, but love. Love in personal relationships among Christians, and between Christians and the rest of the world, and preeminently Christianity itself values a relationship of love between us and God. So do Christians actually enjoy such relationships? Let's find out.

Psychological and Experiential Grounds

Christianity—like all religions—includes an affective dimension. It makes a difference in how one feels. Christianity's central dynamic is walking with God (Micah 6:8), following Jesus, enjoying the indwelling of the Holy Spirit. These are *experiences*. To be true to its promises, Christianity needs to register consistently in this crucial zone of experience: not just in the occasional dramatic encounter with the divine, but in fruitful, faithful daily life. Otherwise, Christianity becomes something else: perhaps moralism, as Christians follow the rules and tick off items on the ethical checklist; or an intriguing worldview within which to pursue ratiocination about matters great and small; or an ideology used to justify individual or corporate activism—or perhaps mere mischief. But Christianity is focused on *life*, on *flourishing*, and in the Christian view this shalom stems from each Christian enjoying a personal relationship of respect and love with God. If Christianity is what it says it is, Christians should be experiencing God importantly and regularly.

Do we?

Let's start modestly, with the proposal that Christianity provides meaning, and thus helps us feel good about our lives when we live them well. The Christian faith frames the entirety of our lives. Most of us feel better when we have a sense of location and direction, when we orient our lives toward an important goal and participate in an important project. And no project could be greater than working with God in the re-creation of shalom in the world. It is a vision that embraces all the noble efforts of all people, Christian or otherwise.[57]

Christianity makes sense of the world. The Christian Story is a narrative in which each person can locate himself or herself in the sweep of history, and can see both backward and forward for a sense of context and purpose. Christians have some sense, even if not anything like a detailed understanding, of what the world is, where we are in the flow of time, who we are meant to be, and where it's all headed. Good and evil, the temporary and the eternal, the physical and the spiritual, the beautiful and the ugly (or the merely ordinary)—the Christian religion speaks to all of these dimensions of life and sets them in a coherent pattern.

This pattern makes sense of both our aspirations and our fears: from the nascent shalom in Eden, to its ancient corruption, through the long process of salvation, to the final fruition of lasting shalom. We long for immortality, we ache over our sins, we grieve over our losses, we mourn for the dead, we aspire to significance— these feelings, so deep and so upsetting that we usually acknowledge them only in life's most extreme experiences, are not delusions to be shed but intimations of fundamental realities we should pay attention to and explore.[58] We may seek, and we often do seek, to fill these holes in our psyches with sex or money or friendships or power or work or family. Or we deny them, lock them away, cut them off, and destroy authentic parts of our deepest selves. "Our hearts are restless, until they find their rest in thee," Augustine prayed. Blaise Pascal recognized the "God-shaped vacuum" in every person's heart, a vacuum that sucks in everything we use to stop it and yet remains unfilled. Christianity says, "Yes!" to our desire to live forever, "Yes!" to our recognition that we are currently unfit to live forever, "Yes!" to our need for forgiveness and restoration, "Yes!" to our permanent attachment to loved ones, "Yes!" to our ambition to count for something that lasts, and "Yes!" to our fundamental feeling that we are, in fact, utterly dependent upon God—and that is just right. The Bible says that in Jesus Christ, "every one of God's promises is a 'Yes' " (2 Corinthians 1:20). At the heart's core, Christianity makes sense.[59]

Christianity therefore provides hope. In the face of confusion, resistance, and even the apparent defeat of our best efforts and highest aspirations, Jesus promises that good will triumph over evil; that our struggles are not in vain; and that, despite appearances, we truly are progressing toward a certain victory: the triumph of the kingdom of God on earth. It is worth getting up in the morning. It is worth each day's labor, whether marked by setbacks or successes. We walk and work with others, step by step, increment by increment, toward the guaranteed goal of peace. Moreover, our sense of meaning and hope is based on our feeling that we are forgiven by God for our many sins and our sense of being welcomed into God's own family. We can look forward with joy to the future because God, at great cost, has freed us from our past. Christianity provides *grounds* to believe that all of these good feelings correspond to realities.[60]

Beyond these feelings of well-being and the benefit of a strong sense of direction, however, Christianity offers spiritual, or mystical, experiences of God. It doesn't just happen to do so, as a kind of interesting, if perhaps unnerving, bonus. The guidance and strength enjoyed in prayer are essential to the Christian way of life, as that life is paradigmatically lived as a partnership between oneself and God. Human beings function optimally in constant communion with our Maker, not off on our own "as gods," deciding for ourselves what is "good and evil." And the Christian way is one of learning how to connect and reconnect with God throughout the day so as to learn to see God in one's peripheral vision, so to speak: to walk through life with the constant sense of God's constant presence—a presence of love, holiness, and creativity, a presence offering power to live as we ought.[61]

Given this understanding of Christian life, shouldn't reports of mystical experience be not just plentiful, but universal? Soul-shaking experiences of the *mysterium tremendum*, reported around the world, deserve serious attention. What prompts them? What are we to make of them?[62] Most of us, however, haven't had such experiences. I have no expertise in discussing them, and Christianity doesn't promise them to everyone, or even most of us. Let's leave the mystics on their mountaintops, therefore, and turn to Christian parents washing dishes, Christian nurses tending patients, Christian salespeople sorting stock, and Christian pilots landing aircraft. Christianity would entail that all of *these* believers should be experiencing God being with *them*, helping them with the guidance and energy they need to live the best life they can and to bless others as they do.

Generally speaking, Christians experience God most vividly through worship and through encounter with other people. Sometimes we sense God's presence as we pray or sing or read Scripture on our own. Sometimes while in church we feel personally addressed by a hymn lyric or a sermonic illustration, or moved by a beautiful window or chord progression. Other times, we sense God reaching out to us through others, and particularly, although not exclusively, through fellow believers: in a comment or question that seems acutely apposite to our current musings, or a gesture that reassures us in a way startlingly relevant to our immediate need, or a kindness that goes well beyond what is expected. All of these moments testify to God's abundant affection for us. In extraordinary times, to be sure, people hear God speak audibly, and even less commonly see Jesus in a vision.[63] But such evidently supernatural occurrences are rare, just as any other sort of miracle is rare (which is what makes them miraculous). God normally works through normal life, and part of growing as a Christian is learning to recognize God meeting us and blessing us in the quotidian.

This can all seem to be mere wish fulfillment and the product of suggestion. Coincidences might be divine doings or they may be just coincidences. Sensible Christians cultivate a healthy skepticism about claims that "God told me that you are to marry me" or "Jesus wants me to have this car I apparently cannot afford." Christians recognize the reality of self-delusion and add to that the peril of demonic delusion as well. So Christians, of all people, ought to be wary of over-claiming when it comes to spiritual experiences.

Christians therefore have developed guidelines to help us discern the leading of God from other inclinations we might feel. Scripture is key: God doesn't contradict Godself, and if I think God is somehow exempting me from the Bible's morality (I am the "special case" every adulterer or cheat thinks he is), I need to think again. The global Church through the ages—what Christians call "the universal Church"—is key also. It is theoretically possible, yes, that I have a special revelation from God that differs from what Christians through the centuries have understood God to say—but I have an awfully large burden of proof to meet if I make this claim. Suffice it to say, it's the very rare person who meets that burden, and most of us do well to walk by the wisdom of our forebears. And the local church is key as well. God works with what God has to work with, and while local churches are always fallible, if they aren't truly pathological (as some, alas, are), God will guide us through their collective wisdom. (Why would God *not* do that? What else should God do to forestall every Christian being left each to his or her own devices about everything, and especially about the vagaries of spiritual life?) Christians therefore do not identify God with just any emotional flutter or even any strong impulse. Quite the contrary. Christians, if they are wise, take serious measures to discern whether God is truly present in this or that experience.

Most of the time, however, we Christians don't feel we are being told something extraordinary by God such that we have to be wary of it. Most of the time we are being reminded of what we have already been taught, and we are being empowered to believe it and to respond appropriately. And while much of that process is plainly cognitive (remembering and applying truth already learned) and volitional (choosing to trust and obey), Christians seek help from the Holy Spirit of God to believe more clearly and firmly, and to respond more gladly and faithfully. (Sometimes, of course, recalling and then doing the right thing is hard, and Christians properly call on God for assistance.)

Therefore, if Christians are truly to walk with God, following Jesus, according to the promptings of the Holy Spirit—well, that's inescapably mystical talk. And Christians, shy as many of us are to speak about it, really do believe that we walk and talk with God all the time.[64]

If you get us to open up, Christians will say that God seems to touch a person inside with the reality of divine presence—daily, not just on high holy occasions. God provides peace where there is turmoil, comfort where there is pain, companionship where there is loneliness, and joy where there is sorrow or depression. God encourages the anxious, strengthens the weak, stabilizes the flighty, and mobilizes the slothful. For some people, at particular times, God seems palpable, such as when people report feeling held in God's warm, strong arms (sometimes paternal, sometimes maternal, sometimes neither). Sometimes the feeling isn't anthropomorphic, but metaphorical in other ways: like the pouring into the heart of warm, shining honey. Sometimes, as Jewish prophets reported, God's Spirit is a fire in the bones (Jeremiah 20:9; Lamentations 1:13). A few people have visions, a few hear a voice, a few feel seized by a kinetic excitement and dance or shout or collapse and tremble on the floor. Depending on one's personality, need, and occasion, God's spiritual wind will blow differently through the aeolian harp of one's soul. But the Spirit does blow through all who open themselves to God. Christianity is not just about believing this and doing that. It is about the whole person in relationship, and thus deeply involves the affective dimension of our being as well.

I was intrigued to read, decades ago now, two volumes of the religious testimonies of an unusual group of people: analytic philosophers. If any demographic on the planet would be convinced by force of reason to convert from one outlook to another, surely it would be such people. But that's not the story they cumulatively tell.[65]

Yes, good arguments for the Christian faith (and, sometimes, against its rivals) played an important part in the journey of many of them. But in not one case did these professional thinkers say that professional thinking had caused them to convert. Instead, a combination of experiences, including obviously mystical ones, drew them in.

Peter van Inwagen is a heavyweight member of this group. The John Cardinal O'Hara Professor of Philosophy at the University of Notre Dame, he has given the Wilde Lectures at Oxford, the Stewart Lectures at Princeton, and the Gifford Lectures at St. Andrews. A member of the American Academy of Arts and Sciences, he is a former president of the American Philosophical Association. He is, in short, a philosopher's philosopher.

As a graduate student, van Inwagen read C. S. Lewis and found himself deeply impressed by the orthodox Christianity Lewis presented. It was much more substantial than the thin soup of liberal theology he had been served in his Unitarian upbringing. And yet—it didn't convert him:

> The only thing was, I didn't believe it. I could see that there was an "it" to believe, and if I did not really see how much there was to being Christian beyond having certain beliefs, I did see that the beliefs must come first, and that a Christian life without those beliefs is an impossibility. One day . . . , I fell to my knees and prayed for faith, but faith did not come. I do not know what led me to make this gesture, but presumably there must have been some sort of felt pressure, and presumably this pressure did not long continue. I expect that I had been setting God some sort of test: If You don't give me faith on the spot, I'll conclude that you do not exist or are not interested in me, and that these pressures I've been feeling have some sort of purely natural explanation and can be ignored till they go away. We all know how well that sort of thing works.[66]

Van Inwagen then says that about a decade later,

> I began to experience a sort of pressure to become a Christian: a vast discontent with *not* being a Christian, a pressure to *do something*. Presumably this pressure was of the same sort that had led me to pray for faith on that one occasion ten years earlier, but

this was sustained. This went on and on. . . . I perhaps did not have anything like a desire to turn to Christ as my Saviour, or a desire to lead a godly, righteous, and sober life [van Inwagen is alluding to the Anglican/Episcopalian *Book of Common Prayer*], but I did have a strong desire to belong to a Christian community of discourse.[67]

Van Inwagen eventually asks another philosopher, the estimable William Alston (himself a one-time president of the American Philosophical Association from whom we will hear more in a moment), to put him in touch with a priest. Alston does so; van Inwagen starts going to church; and a couple of years later (not days or weeks—*years*), van Inwagen is baptized. Reflecting on these experiences, van Inwagen confesses, "What it was about those prayers that was different from my [earlier] prayer, or what it was that I did besides prayer, is unknown to me."[68] This is hardly a story of philosophical inference to the best explanation, and yet van Inwagen has remained a professed—and powerfully articulate—Christian ever since.

William Alston shares a similar story in turn about multiple events and factors occurring along his way that brought him eventually to a convinced faith. Alston begins his narrative quite unphilosophically:

It was certainly not that I had become convinced of the truth of Christianity by philosophical, theological, or historical arguments. It was largely a matter of feeling a church-shaped hole in my life and having sufficient motivation to fill it. I believe that I went into the Episcopal church with the idea that "I'll give it a fling and see what's there" rather than "I am thoroughly convinced that this is the right story, and therefore the thing to do is to sign up."[69]

This first attempt at experiencing Christianity didn't "take" for Alston. Only a quarter-century later, having had "a lot" of psychotherapy that helped him "hear the gospel message straight or more nearly straight," did Alston return to Christianity.[70] Yet psychotherapy had also put a barrier in his way. "The main bar to faith was . . . the Freudian idea that religious faith is wish fulfillment—more specifically, an attempt to cling to childish modes of relating to the world, with the omnipotent daddy presiding over everything."[71] This humiliating version of Christian belief haunted Alston until, one day, he had a revelation:

> The crucial moment in my return to the faith came quite early in that year's leave, before I had re-exposed myself to the church or the Bible, or even thought seriously about the possibility of becoming a Christian. I was walking one afternoon in the country outside Oxford, wrestling with the problem, when I suddenly said to myself, "Why should I allow myself to be cribbed, cabined, and confined by these Freudian ghosts? Why should I be so afraid of not being adult? What am I trying to prove? Whom am I trying to impress? Whose approval am I trying to secure? What is more important: to struggle to conform my life to the tenets of some highly speculative system of psychology or to recognize and come to terms with my own real needs? Why should I hold back from opening myself to a transcendent dimension of reality, if such there be, just from fear of being branded as childish in some quarters?" . . . These questions answered themselves as soon as they were squarely posed. I have, by the grace of God, finally found the courage to look the specter in the face and tell him to go away. I had been given the courage to face the human situation, with its radical need for proper relation to the source of all being.[72]

When Alston returned to the United States, he was even then not fully a Christian, by his own estimation. What confirmed for him that something new had emerged in his life was his growing interest in caring for other people. "I began, for the first time in my life, to get a glimmer of what love means. It was a most exhilarating experience. Just to make sure that I was not imagining all this, I checked with my wife, my main contact with external reality. She assured me that I was, indeed, quite different." Alston then attended church (in Princeton) and came under the influence of a capable preacher. "One not only heard the gospel being interpreted in a way that had direct application to one's situation then and there, but one could, as it were, literally see the gospel being lived out in front of one. All this without any obvious histrionics and with the aid of profound scholarship. . . . [This preacher] is a living example of what Christian spirituality can be in [modern] America." Alston's own scholarship in the philosophy of religion, some of it cited elsewhere in this chapter, has been crucial in modern philosophy. Yet he himself was not argued into the faith. "So far as I am aware, it was primarily a process of responding to a call, of being drawn into a community, into a way of life. . . . I found the vertical dimension through the horizontal. I found God as a reality in my life through finding a community of faith and being drawn into it."[73]

It isn't as if rational grounds to believe don't matter. As we have established, one cannot believe by a sheer act of will. One believes that what one has concluded deserves belief, what one thinks is true and trustworthy. And if one has prior questions about the plausibility or credibility of Christianity, one deserves adequate answers. But Christianity is not the correct result of a proof, the necessary outcome of a lab experiment, the inevitable conclusion of a chain of inference. It is a comprehensive explanation of the universe, yes, but it is also a way of negotiating that universe in the company of people who share Christian views and Christian values, a company of people who, we believe, are inhabited by the Holy Spirit of God. There are good grounds to believe that Christianity is true—real and good and beautiful—but to *see* that it is *and then* to embrace not only Christianity the religion, but Jesus Christ the Person, is a matter transcending argument, a matter squarely in the realm of the experiential, intuitive, and ethical.[74]

So now we have summarized the grounds of Christian faith—why at least some people, and in fact upward now of two billion people, believe the extraordinary and unlikely religion centered on Jesus of Nazareth. Not every kind of ground is equally important to each believer, of course. Many, perhaps, are strongly persuaded by only one or two. But the thoughtful inquirer ought to be apprised of the full gamut of possibly interesting and convincing grounds, so here's the best roundup I can offer.[75]

And yet questions remain. Some of them are rather secondary, but others are pretty important. In the next chapter, we look at two of the most important reasons *not* to believe.

4

Why Not Believe?

The Problem of Particularity

In this era of inter-religious tensions, which in some countries have erupted into open warfare, one might think it would be politically expedient to claim that all religions are basically the same. (By "religions" here we continue to include philosophies of all sorts, as we persist in using "religion" in a *functional* sense.) If we can somehow come to believe that all the major religions, at least, reduce to some basic combination of virtues (compassion, say, plus honesty, industriousness, loyalty, magnanimity, mutual respect, and the like), then surely we can all get along reasonably well. There would no doubt remain the ignorantly recalcitrant who cling to their particularity and insist on their superiority, but those of us belonging to the moral consensus can band together to deal with those difficult ones.

I celebrate any ethical common ground there might be with any of my neighbors and, having taught introductory courses in world religions for thirty years, I gratefully recognize the virtues that many of the world's religions share. Without such shared values, multicultural societies like my own in Canada could not exist. Those of us who share moral values *do* need to recognize each other and work together toward what we all can agree is the common good. Likewise, we *do* need to resist, if we cannot convert, those who insist on their own peculiar rightness if they threaten the common social project.[1]

Still, it must be recognized that religions and philosophies say different things and offer different things. Some people stop here to suggest that the fact of all of these people giving so many different answers to the same big questions must mean that none of them have the right answers. That is a curious conclusion, however. A mathematics teacher grading her tests doesn't normally conclude that all of her students must be wrong merely because lots of them give lots of different answers. Our New Atheist friends contend that science gives us *real knowledge*, as evidenced by the global consensus on scientific facts. Religion clearly does not, they say, as evidenced by the global disagreement on even basic religious tenets. In this context, we do well to recognize two main points.

First, the major religions of the world do in fact agree on a number of crucial ideas, especially in the realm of morality; second, it should not surprise us that there will be less consensus in the realm of religion than in science. Philosopher William Alston suggests why:

> Why shouldn't there be realms, modes, or dimensions of reality that are so difficult for us to discern that widespread agreement is extremely difficult or impossible to attain, even if *some* veridical cognition of that realm is achieved? It is a familiar fact that the more difficult the task, the more widely dispersed the attempts to carry it out. This holds in areas as diverse as mathematical exercises and target practice. Why should it be surprising that attempts to discern the Ultimate Source of all being should vary so much, even if some of those attempts get it straight?[2]

The great religions really do differ across each major category of belief and practice. They do not all offer the same God or gods—or any deity at all. They do not all offer the same views of good and evil, the same appraisal of the human condition, the same answers to human questions, and the same solutions to human problems. They tell different stories, make different claims, and offer different promises. Similar as some religions and philosophies undoubtedly are to some others in some respects, they are not reducible (as many people suppose) to a "lowest common denominator." They disagree too deeply about too much. Nor is it obvious how some great synthesis could bring their "best" elements together (an idea that has intrigued thoughtful people throughout the ages, and especially in our time) without compromising their essential characters—and without those "best" elements amounting in fact to no more than a generalized expression of the individual synthesizer's own preferences.[3]

Christianity, as we have seen, makes extraordinarily particular claims. Rather than commending its view of things by showing how Christianity corresponds to general intuitions about the world (although one might do that with some success among some audiences), Christianity rather scandalously plunks down its very particular narrative and says, "Here. Here is the Story we all must understand, accept as true, and live by. Here is the one Person at the heart of everything. No matter what else you have believed, no matter what other path you have walked, no matter whom else you have followed, you need to adopt this Story as the guiding narrative of your life. You need to adopt this path as your way of life. And you need to adopt this Person as the Center of your life."[4]

Christianity thus doesn't just surprise. It offends. It disrupts. It scandalizes—a word that stems from the Greek skandalon, a term for an impediment so significant that it causes one to stumble. The gospel itself, according to the apostle Paul, is just such a "stumbling block" (1 Corinthians 1:23). The so-called scandal of particularity in Christianity comes to us in at least three successive forms: (1) the scandal of Christianity's focus on Jesus, as above the founders of all other religions; (2) the scandal of Christian missions, the worldwide project of Christians using any means they can think of to convert their families, friends, neighbors, and even strangers to their faith—no matter how noble the religion those people are currently practicing or how well they are practicing it; and (3) the scandal of Christianity's insistence that salvation can be had only by acceding to this missionary enterprise and believing in Jesus—with the horrible entailment that those who do not hear, understand, and believe this message are destined for eternal torment in hell. Let's take these three scandals in turn. We may find that Christianity can be less scandalous than it appears, but still scandalous nevertheless.

First, Jesus versus other religions' founders. We can reduce the scandal, but not eliminate it, by reminding ourselves of what Christianity actually says and being careful to note what it doesn't say. The Christian Story says that Jesus was Israel's long-awaited Messiah, the Special One appointed by God. *Mashiach* in Hebrew means "an anointed one"—a person with sacred oil ritually placed on his head as a sign of God's commissioning, whether king, priest, or prophet. This supreme Messiah, so to speak, was commissioned to save God's people and, by extension, the world. The gospel outlines the life of Jesus, focusing on his public career, with extended attention to its dramatic termination in his suffering, death, burial, and resurrection—events that, the gospel explains, procured salvation for all humanity. As the Divine-Human One, the gospel says, Jesus completed this stage of his earthly work (he will return someday for the next stage) and ascended to heaven to take the seat of authority over the world and particularly over the Church, which is why the early Church confessed that "*Jesus is Lord*" as well as being the *Savior*.[5]

I recall giving lectures on this subject to Ph.D. students in Chinese universities. They were scratching their heads over Christianity's audacious insistence on the superiority of Jesus over their great sages, such as Laozi and Kongzi. They could see why we Christians venerated Jesus as a similarly wise master. But why would we claim to respect their traditions, as we did, only to champion Jesus as the One Savior and Lord?

It was gratifying to see the light dawn as I explained that the logic of the Christian Story *requires* there to be a Savior who must also be the Lord. Only God can take on Godself the suffering of the whole human race, while only God-in-human-form can stand in such solidarity with humanity. So if Jesus of Nazareth is truly this instance of incarnation, of God becoming human, and if Jesus subsequently does those things necessary to procure the salvation of the world—through an innocent life, dreadful suffering, actual death and burial, and genuine resurrection—then ipso facto Jesus is the Savior. And given that this Savior is the Supreme Being and capable of setting right what is wrong, the world doesn't need 5, or 26, or 114 more saviors. We need just one. Moreover, such a Savior must be the one and only God, so it follows that Jesus is the one and only Lord.

There is plenty of room within Christianity's capacious embrace to respect the wisdom of Laozi, Kongzi, and the rest of the world's great teachers. But Jesus isn't being championed by Christians as if he were the smartest scholar in the seminar, or the nicest guy in the fraternity, or the noblest soul in the world. Christians don't believe that Jesus is the best among a set of similar elements. He is held up as the one and only Savior because Christianity—remember, a religion completely focused on history, on what happened— believes Jesus did what needed doing. No other religious leader in the world has even *attempted* to suffer and die for the sins of humanity, let alone try to defeat death by coming back to life. No other religion claims anything like this for their founder: not Hinduism about Krishna, not Buddhism about Siddhartha Gautama, not Islam about Muhammad, not Confucianism about Kongzi. Only Christianity does, and it does so because it is in the very logic of Christianity to do so. Christians *have* to say that Jesus is Savior and Lord if we are to claim for Jesus what the entire Christian Story implies is true about him. If Christians say anything else, anything less, then we have failed to grasp correctly our own religion. The whole Christian Story has to be rewritten into a quite different religion. As Søren Kierkegaard put it, Jesus *has* to be "the sign of offense in order to be the object of faith."[6]

In sum, Christianity might be *wrong* about Jesus being Savior and Lord. But Christianity isn't being *arbitrary* in its claims about Jesus. The whole Christian Story builds to the climax of God becoming human in order to save the world, and once that Divine-Human Person has done so, it only follows that he is to be recognized as the one Savior needed and worshipped as the one legitimate Lord.

Thus the scandal remains and cannot be avoided: Christianity claims that its founder is not so much "The Best" as *The Only*. Such a claim isn't religious chauvinism, but is actually required by the logic of Christianity's central Story. We Christians might be wrong about Jesus. Maybe we have identified the wrong person as Messiah. Maybe the whole Christian Story is invalid, or at least badly composed and in dire need of revision. But I hope it now makes sense why we say what we say about him. We have to.

The second scandal here is that we Christians not only believe this extremely particular, even narrow, idea—that there is one Savior and Lord and we know who he is—but we insist on telling other people about him. Not only that, which might be excused as sheer enthusiasm, as one indulges a friend who raves about a newly discovered wine or TV show, but we Christians actively try to persuade people away from whatever beliefs and values and lifestyle they have chosen, or been born into, and to embrace Jesus and Christianity and the Christian way of life. We do so because we believe that if people don't do so, they are in peril of forfeiting the best of this world and all of the next.

Entertainer and outspoken atheist Penn Jillette sees the logic here:

> I've always said, you know, that I don't respect people who don't proselytize. I don't respect that at all. If you believe that there's a heaven and hell, and people could be going to hell, or not getting eternal life, or whatever, and you think that, "Well, it's not really worth tellin' 'em this, because it would make it socially awkward," and atheists who think that people shouldn't proselytize—"Just leave me alone. Keep your religion to yourself"—How much do you have to hate somebody to not proselytize? How much do you have to hate somebody to believe that everlasting life is possible

and not tell them that? I mean, if I believed, beyond a shadow of a doubt, that a truck was coming at you and you didn't believe it—that truck was bearing down on you—there's a certain point where I tackle you, and this is more important than that.[7]

What Jillette sees is what many people in our multicultural societies don't: that accommodating each other's religious differences means, among other things, accommodating the fact that lots of people fervently believe that lots of other people should convert to their way of thought and life. We accommodate proselytizing—let's call it what it is—in economic and political discussions all the time. We do the same about a wide range of social and environmental issues as well—from sex and gender to global climate change. In fact, we positively *expect* people to try to persuade others to change their minds about those things. Great matters are at stake, and doing all you legitimately can to bring people over to your side is entirely normal. Somehow, however, we're still finding our way toward accommodating each other's advocacy regarding The Most Important Issues of All.

One might concede that the imperative to share the gospel with others makes sense. But what about the third scandal, the Christian conviction that to be saved a person has to have heard, understood, and accepted the Bible's account of Jesus's life, suffering, death, resurrection, and ascension—in short, to have believed the gospel? What about the millions of people over the millennia of human history who have never heard this Story, through no fault of their own? Are they all doomed?

Lots of Christians have thought so. Many a missionary career has been launched by the horrific image of a "Niagara of souls" plunging into a lost eternity for lack of hearing the gospel. But Christians don't have to think this way, and many of us don't.

Instead, let's notice something that many Christians have yet to notice in their own New Testament—the explicitly Christian part of the Bible (the Old Testament being, of course, the Hebrew Bible accepted by the early Christians as scripture). These Christian scriptures hold up as models of faith many *Old* Testament believers who, ipso facto, did not know the story of Jesus—since he had yet to be born. In fact, a key chapter of the New Testament, Hebrews 11, sets out for the inspiration of Christian believers a whole gallery of faithful people, not one of whom could possibly have heard of Jesus, since the list is drawn from the Old Testament. And remember, this is a Christian book in the Christian New Testament written by a Christian author for a Christian audience.

Hebrews 11 is prefaced by a definition of faith: "Without faith it is impossible to please God, for whoever would approach him must believe that he exists and that he rewards those who seek him" (11:6). So anyone who (1) believes that God exists—and Romans 1:19–21 makes it clear that God has shown everyone that God exists—and (2) trusts God to be good to us if we will turn to God meets the definition of faith. That person's actual understanding of God might be shadowy and distorted indeed, as Christian theologians believe is true of, say, a Muslim believer or a Hindu devotee of Vishnu, or, frankly, a typical North American Christian! But whoever actually encounters God (as the Holy Spirit can make possible for anyone, anywhere) and responds in humble trust meets the criteria of this famous Biblical chapter on faith.

I am not espousing the popular view that God is happy to bless anyone who is sincere in whatever he or she believes. God is not pleased with sincere racism, or sincere sexism, or the sincere worship of dark divinities whose values are at cross purposes with God's. People must respond positively to whatever vision they have received of the *true* God, however conceptually deficient that understanding might be at the moment. But if they do respond in faith to God—again, this isn't a matter of assenting to certain correct doctrines about the divine, but of responding personally to a mystical encounter with the true God—then God receives them gladly.

I have to say, therefore, that the traditional view (I was taught it myself) that people must explicitly hear, understand, and receive the Jesus Story—must receive and properly process this information—smacks of magic. "Only this spell, learned and then recited verbatim, will produce the desired results." It also raises all sorts of thorny questions: How accurately does one have to understand the gospel? What score would one have to achieve on a divinely mandated theology quiz? What, then, about children, or people with mental disorders, or people trying to understand the gospel through very different worldviews, or people whose previous experience of the Christian religion has been abusive? Must they get every element of the gospel message straight, to the satisfaction of a theologian, before they can be assured of their salvation? The understanding of faith I'm setting out here is consistent with the Bible's own portrayal of person after person, in the Old Testament and the New, who simply could not have had a very rich and accurate conception of God, let alone a properly framed understanding of Jesus, and yet is clearly accepted by God on the basis of what they do demonstrate: faith in (the true) God.

Then why do Christians persist in missionary work? Why do we keep telling people about Jesus as often and as persuasively as we can? Is there yet another scandal here? Are Christians bothering people to no purpose, perhaps needlessly confronting them, even putting them in danger (as is true in many parts of the world today) by asking them to leave their current religion to become Christians?

Even if what I have suggested is true—that God meets people all over the world through whatever confused or partial view of the Supreme Being they currently possess and calls them to put their trust in the true God they have thus encountered—Christian missions yet have much to offer. The Christian vision of life, of course, is not restricted to the binary idea of "in/out," "born again or not." Evangelism is not merely a membership drive. The Christian life is a process of maturation, of growing up to be a properly formed adult (Colossians 1:28), and so perforce each convert would benefit greatly from being introduced to the Bible and the Church as soon and as well as possible. More basically, though, God becomes much more attractive when clearly distinguished from the world's confused portraits of the divine and made available instead in the image of God's Son, Jesus Christ. So hearing the good news about Jesus would make coming to faith in God much easier, even as enjoying the Bible and the Church would dramatically contribute to one's growing up correctly. So Christian missions are hardly pointless. Instead, these ideas both reframe their value and remove what to some is a serious obstacle to faith—namely, the terrible idea that God doesn't care about, or somehow cannot do anything about, all those people whom Christians haven't yet reached with their evangelism.[8]

Perhaps, then, you will agree that, at least by their own lights, it makes sense for Christians to champion Jesus and to commend him to our neighbors around the world. But lurking in the shadows is a darkness that threatens to extinguish all this light and life: the problem of evil. How can Christians believe, let alone urge others to believe, in an all-good, all-powerful God when we are surrounded by and submerged in so much evil in the world?

The Problem of Evil

The problem of evil—how an all-powerful, all-good God can allow evil in creation—is a problem not only for inquirers but for believers.

We might pause to note that it's not obvious why atheists, or people who believe only in some vague spiritual energy in the cosmos, are horrified by wickedness. No sane person likes the idea of cruelty or any other unmerited suffering, of course. But to judge other human beings as *evil* requires belief that there exists an objective standard of good and evil sufficiently recognizable to enable a valid verdict on someone else. Such a belief is not available from science, which can only describe what is, not prescribe what ought to be, and stems instead from the moral values one gets from—well, from what? Or Whom? The Christian at least has grounds to make moral judgments, even judgments about the behavior of God. The atheist, or the vaguely spiritual, has difficulty articulating a cogent reason for her or his own moral convictions.

Throughout the Bible itself, believers are shown to be perplexed, even frustrated and angry, not only with evildoers but with *God*. The Book of Job is the classic statement of such dismay, but many other Old Testament worthies—Moses, the great King David, the prophet Jeremiah—complain directly to God *about* God. And the New Testament writers feel obliged constantly to offer reassurance to Christians that, despite undeniable evidence to the contrary, God is at work, Jesus is in fact Lord of all, and all will be well. The problem of evil is a big problem for faith.

Ironically, in the Bible itself God sometimes seems to tolerate and even command evil, particularly (but not exclusively) in the Old Testament: from Abraham being commanded to sacrifice his son (even if God granted him a last-minute reprieve); to the ten plagues of Egypt (which struck powerful and poor alike); to the very laws of God given at Mount Sinai, which include draconian punishment for a range of offenses that shock modern sensibilities; to the violent clearing of the Promised Land; to God striking dead *Christians* who lied about their charitable giving, of all things (Acts 5:1–11). Christians have offered a range of explanations and defenses for all those scriptural horrors, as have Jews (from whom we inherited the Hebrew Bible). But the point for us now is simple: *There's a problem here.*

I offer the modest suggestion, therefore, that if the greatest believers depicted in the Bible didn't arrive at a neat and satisfactory solution to the problem of evil, and if the Bible itself doesn't offer us a nicely packaged explanation, you're not likely to get one from this book either. But we can at least account for how modern believers somehow keep faith in God despite the pervasive reality of evil throughout our world.

Indeed, the real problem is precisely keeping faith in God. Theoretically, God could give us full knowledge of all God's doings and we then wouldn't have to have faith. We would simply see, understand, and approve of God's providence.

It seems extremely doubtful, however, that we human beings have the intellectual capacity to take in God's global providence over millennia (quite a few data points there, with a considerable number of decision branches to mull over) plus the moral capacity to make correct judgments. ("Ah! Yes, I see now that that *was* a difficult trade-off: But good for you, God! You called it right. Okay, let's look at the next one. . . .") To believe in general terms, as we should, that the world is not at all as it should be is not the same as having justified confidence in our ability to determine exactly how the greatest good would be produced in any given situation.

Nonetheless, God cannot simply *demand* that we trust what God's doing. Faith doesn't work that way. We need knowledge to ground faith. To keep trusting in God's goodness and power in the face of the teeming evil of the world requires quite a lot of knowledge. In the brief space we have here in which to consider this huge question (I have addressed it at book-length elsewhere), we can sketch the outline of what grounds Christians have indeed found for faith and trust in God.[9]

First, this obviously bad world can paradoxically be seen as also a good world after all. By "good" here I mean "optimally productive of the optimal outcome." Most of us would agree that if the test of a good world is a world that produces universal happiness, this world is a dreadful failure. But a world suffused with a free and potent narcotic in which everyone passed their time, and eventually passed away, in a pleasant opioid slumber is hardly what we would call an optimally good world. So the fact that our world often produces something other than happiness—even in a more general utilitarian sense—is not immediately a mark against God's good administration of it.

Our actual world, by contrast, is a world that was created for human beings to enjoy cultivating, and it still is such a world. At the same time, because of the Fall, we human beings often make messes where we should create improvements, and these messes are symptomatic of our mortal moral disease, which the Bible calls *sin*. This good world performs the vital service of showing us the consequences—what we sometimes in fact call the "real-world consequences"—of our inward state. No matter what clever schemes and grand regimes we set up, we keep making a mess. We don't make only messes, of course. The image of God in us, that creative resemblance to the divine Creator's creativity, continues to motivate us to shalom. But we also seem completely unable si-multaneously to maximize even a few key values, such as equality, freedom, security, and comfort. The world keeps showing us that inability—indeed, that frequent unwillingness—to achieve unmit-igated goodness. To render that diagnosis regularly and vividly is crucially helpful.

At the same time, the world also provides us opportunities to grow up: to improve and to be improved. God has provided us both with moral wisdom such that we do at least dimly see the path of life and with moral communities to help us make progress along it. Indeed, having been given a fresh start through faith in the true God and regeneration by God's Holy Spirit, the world then provides the resources and opportunities to practice virtue and become ma-ture people who are finally fit to enjoy the glories of the world to come. The world therefore seems brilliantly designed to help us as we actually are to move toward an optimal future.

Now wait just a second, the patient reader might exclaim. A lot of these "opportunities to grow up" *hurt*. A lot of these "moral communities" are infested with wickedness, if one can find such a community nearby at all. And a lot of people clearly don't be-come better as they negotiate life's challenges, but worse: more angry, more bitter, more abusive. So it's not like the actual world is some sort of spa, or a rehab facility, or even a well-run boot camp.

A lot of it seems more like a war zone. I cannot disagree, of course. Christians are looking for the method in the apparent madness. And millions of us have come to believe that the world is a place well designed to produce goodness, even greatness, even as many people choose to respond to it instead with ever-increasing evil, or just cynical despair. The world sorts us out.

Suffering in Christian terms therefore is paradoxically both denied—it is intrinsically bad and it will not last forever: it will not exist in the world to come—and validated. It makes a certain, limited sense in God's cosmos; it plays an important role, and suffering thus *means something*, even if the meaning is often opaque to us.

Why, however, didn't God just make us perfect—mature, complete—in the first place? Why does the path to completeness have to start so far back, take so long, and demand so much?

I'm always struck by "Why didn't God just—" questions. The "just" implies that what is being asked for would be no big deal, at least for the Supreme Being. (This type of question often shows up alongside the questioner's presumption that if *he*—and it's usually a "he"—were the Supreme Being, by God, he would have done things properly: say, from a Christopher Hitchens, for example.)[10]

What is at stake is, in fact, usually a rather large deal, if not an impossibility. God cannot "just" do anything we think we can imagine, let alone merely state. "Why didn't God just make a square circle?" is a nonsense question. Even the Supreme Being can't manufacture a contradiction. "Why didn't God just create morally mature free-will beings?" may be a similar question. It's not identical to the square circle: it isn't a flat contradiction, at least to our sensibilities. But to instantly create a morally mature free-will being may yet be ipso facto impossible. It may be that there is no such thing, that there can be no such thing as a creature instantly created who possesses strong virtues, with a constant appetite for goodness and zero appetite for sin who yet also possesses free will—which is the state toward which we aspire and that is promised us in the Bible. Perhaps such a creature can emerge only from a process of maturation, with experiences and habits that over a long time and with considerable effort produce a strong character, as well as the memories to keep one on the straight and narrow. God might make a creature that *looked* like that, but I wonder if it would be merely a simulacrum, a moral robot whose virtue wasn't "earned," wasn't organically produced and therefore authentic—including authentically *free*.

God loves the world and wants its best. This love naturally entails wanting God's beloved to suffer as little as possible. God hates evil of all sorts and in every degree. And God can do anything God wants to do *that can be done*. Surely God would choose the shortest and easiest path to optimal good. Why multiply suffering? When God's own Son faced his own impending suffering—inconceivable suffering, suffering for the sin of the entire human race—Jesus asked if it was possible that some easier route could be found. He received only an affirmation of the path he was on and so he calmly surrendered himself to the arresting soldiers who would bring him to his doom (Matthew 26:36–46). If God could not find a way to save the world except at the expense of God's own horrible suffering and death, then one can assume God cannot find a way to create, sustain, and shepherd a human race to eventual maturity without going through what we have had to go through. We might *think* God could or should be able to do that, but then God's answer to Job resounds through the centuries: in essence, *You are completely incompetent to make such a judgment: You can't even make a horse* (see Job 39:19–25).

But is that it? Is that all Christians can say to maintain their faith in the face of today's disaster and history's long account of atrocity? And what about "nature red in tooth and claw," the suffering that abounds in the natural world? What do Christians have to say about all that? Only this more or less interesting speculation on the nature of things, the limits of God's power, and the necessity of an ages-long and agonizing process? Is *that* enough to comfort the believer when the latest outrage appears on your news feed or the latest harm afflicts someone near and dear to you? Happily, no. The Christian has much more to go on than these philosophical musings.

Martin Luther is one in the long line of Christian believers who have been puzzled, even dismayed, by the way God runs the world. He received from his theological mentor, Johann Staupitz, some wisdom that he relayed to his own students and to the rest of us too. Staupitz counseled the troubled young Luther to view God's mysterious ways, including the problem of evil, "in the wounds of Christ." The so-called hidden God—the God who administers the world in what sometimes seem to be appalling ways without offering a rationale for them, the God who often allows the innocent to suffer and the wicked to prosper—would never be comprehensible by mere human beings. Indeed, Luther later said to his own students, don't try to climb up and peer into the ways of this God, or you will lose your reason (it will exceed your rational capacity and leave you merely bewildered, or worse) and your faith (you will not be able to comprehend why God can be good and still do what God does, so you will stop loving and trusting God). Staupitz advised Luther to flee this hidden God, this dark, inscrutable Mystery, and *run to Christ*.

At first blush, this prescription seems absurd—and even heretical. It's as if Staupitz believes there are two deities, the bad god who is responsible for this damaged and damaging world and the good god who can be trusted to rescue and restore it. But Staupitz and Luther were orthodox Christians who believed in only one God—only one God, but a *triune* God. Here is one place in which the weird Christian doctrine of the three-in-one God does some useful conceptual work—with benefit, also, to the heart.

Christians, after all, believe that Jesus was good. In fact, most people who encounter Jesus believe that. He freely associates with all sorts of people, refusing to reserve himself only for the religiously observant. He enjoys parties and long walks with friends.

He uses simple, vivid language so as to communicate with everyone who listens. He's even good with kids!

Christians go far beyond this "nice guy Jesus" to aver that Jesus is the very model of properly functioning humanity, the very "Son of Man" who shows us how to live before God and in harmony with the rest of creation. Jesus is the Good Shepherd who gives his life for his sheep. Jesus, yes, is unquestionably good.

Jesus is also, according to the doctrines of Trinity and Incarnation, God. He is not merely an inspired prophet who relays good words from God, nor a saint who exemplifies godliness. He doesn't just speak about God or act on behalf of God: Jesus *is* God. The early Church worshipped Jesus as Lord—something those devout Jews could bring themselves to do only if they equated Jesus with Yahweh, which they did. (Soon, the Holy Spirit they were experiencing and whom Jesus promised as his earthly replacement was likewise recognized as a Person of the divine Trinity.) The following syllogism is a neat one, but it is profound out of all proportion to its concision:

Jesus is good.
Jesus is God.
Therefore, God is good.

The fundamental Christian answer to the ancient problem of evil, therefore, is not high-flown philosophy, however helpful that may be to some, but the answer every Sunday school kid knows to give when you can't think of any other way to respond to a question: *Jesus.* Jesus is the heart of the Christian religion, so of course he is the source of Christian faith. We trust God *because we trust Jesus.* And thus he is the best answer to our own doubts as well as those of interested others.

In the Christian view, if we want to know what God is truly like, we can look at Jesus, for Jesus is God. In Jesus we see what we desperately need to see: God close to us, God active among us, God loving us, God forgiving our sin, God opening up and leading us to a new life of everlasting love. If Jesus is the human face of God, then human beings have a God who cares, a God who acts on our behalf (even to the point of self-sacrifice), and a God who is now engaged in the conquest of evil and the re-establishment of universal shalom for all time. If Jesus is truly God revealed, then we can trust God in spite of the evil all around us and in us.

In the face of evil, God in Jesus declares Godself to us, touches us through the love of others, speaks to us through the Bible and in prayer, and provides for our needs with our ultimate welfare always in view. We can trust God both when we understand at least something of why some evils occur, and also when we feel completely without a clue. All our other questions and challenges can be resolved, or at least endured, if we can be convinced that Jesus, who is indisputably good, is also assuredly God. We can respond properly—with faith and fortitude—to evil in our lives because we know that God is all-good and all-powerful and will eventually and ultimately set everything right. And we know all of that because we know Jesus.

5

What Now?

As William James puts it, what are the "live options" for you?[1] Of course, you can't investigate every extant possibility. So let's deal with what's on the table—your table. How would you give Christianity a serious look—maybe for the first time, maybe as a disaffected ex-Christian willing to give it another go?

As we noted earlier, to properly consider Christianity, you should read an introductory book written by a believer. So far, so good, I trust (!), and there are many other good introductions available besides this one.[2] Then you should move on to read the Bible, preferably in a serious modern translation: the New Revised Standard Version and the New International Version are the market leaders, and either is a good choice. (Most Christians recommend starting with one of the Gospels, rather than on page one of Genesis, so that you immediately get acquainted with Jesus, the center of the story.) You would gain helpful perspective also from a good objective account of Christianity, perhaps in a reliable encyclopedia or textbook on world religions.[3]

Beyond this reading, you should find a good church and get acquainted with the people there who seriously practice the faith. You needn't settle for the first church you visit. There are dull churches just as there are dull versions of anything else. Look for the most attractive, impressive Christians you can find; don't miss a good thing by encountering a bad version of it. And Christianity is expressed in lots of different styles, so you might want to visit a few until you find one that connects with you. Spend some time there, not just attending Sunday mornings but meeting with a small group—most vital churches have them. Here is where committed Christians learn to practice that way of life. Try it on and see for yourself what good might be there for you.

You should also consult critics of Christianity, such as people who have experienced it and left it, or people who have studied it and found fault with it. We test our hypotheses by subjecting them to the strongest critiques available. In sum, let's engage in such exploration as thoroughly and wisely as we can.

This question of "how to decide," however, must be parsed carefully. It can sound as if we are merely opting for our preference: chocolate over vanilla, or hiking shoes over cowboy boots.

There is a sense in which it *is* something like just making our preferred choice. If you want to become immune to the suffering we all encounter in the world, then, yes, you can opt for the detachment of Theravada Buddhism—or the similar *ataraxia* ("imperturbability") of Epicureanism or Stoicism—and, by all accounts, you will eventually experience that. If you want to live a life of moral rectitude, you can opt to follow the Law of Judaism, the shari'ah of Islam, or the wisdom of Confucianism. Devotees of those religions do demonstrate ethical rigor. If you want to sleep with as many people as possible while remaining untroubled by conscience, then the old *Playboy* philosophy (hedonism) is clearly for you. So you can, in this sense, really just pick what you like.

The universe isn't as versatile and pliable as we might like it to be, however. It does not conform to our wishes, or even our most fervent beliefs. Let's suppose we have a Buddhist, a Muslim, and a playboy. Let's suppose that each of them enjoys the fruits of those life philosophies so long as he is alive—but then comes death, what sociologists Peter Berger and Thomas Luckmann describe as "the most terrifying threat to the taken-for-granted realities of everyday life."[4] Upon receiving a prize from the National Book Critics Circle, Margaret Atwood poignantly remarked, "I will cherish this lifetime achievement award from you, though, like all sublunar blessings, it is a mixed one. Why do I only get one lifetime? Where did this life-time go?"[5] Where *does* it go?

Buddhism says that the devotee simply winks out of existence, going where the candle flame goes when the candle is blown out. The Muslim says that the faithful person goes to Paradise, pictured in the Qur'an as a superlative oasis. And for the playboy, a meta-physical materialist (whether he knows it or not) one just stops ex-isting at the moment of brain death.[6]

That's what they say. But whatever lies beyond death *lies beyond death* whether we anticipate it correctly or not. If the Buddhist is right, and really can escape the wheel of suffering endless reincarnations (*samsara*) into the peaceful oblivion of nirvana, then he does—but the Muslim and the playboy are doomed to live again, and again, and again, until they grasp the Four Noble Truths of Buddhism and embark on the Noble Eightfold Path. If the Muslim really does enter Paradise, the Buddhist and the playboy are doomed to suffer the fires of hell, having failed to submit to Allah. And if the playboy really stops existing, so do the other two. The End. Beyond death there is *whatever there is*, regardless of the sincerity of our convictions about it. Not every religion or philos-ophy prepares us equally well to confront whatever there really is beyond death.

Deciding about religion in the light of this great Fact shouldn't be understood as a matter of pursuing one's preferences. It should in-stead be an urgent quest to ascertain reality and respond to it prop-erly. Deciding about religion is not about fulfilling one's wishes, but about discovering and accepting whatever is truly the case. Each of us has the awesome responsibility of deciding about religion. It's not about just picking a god the way a child can pick a doll, or even building one in the right kind of toy store. No, there *are* whatever gods there *are*, and the wise person tries her best to find out what's what and who's who while she still can.

Moreover, until we die we are living each day according to what we assume are true beliefs about the cosmos—true enough, at least, that we think we are negotiating the world as well as we can. We make decisions based on what we take for granted is actually the case: whether love and loyalty are real and can be depended upon (rather than, say, evolutionary reproductive strategies, or ways of scoring points with the Deity in hopes of securing favors from Him/Her/It); whether honesty really is the best policy (versus Machiavelli's or Nietzsche's recommendation of the superior person's tactical ruthlessness); and whether power and wealth should be shared with the needy or concentrated in the hands of those who accrue it. Every morning, we *are* deciding about religion. "This is what I [continue to choose to] believe is true, and good, and beautiful. Thus I shall live this way rather than that."

The universe, though, is however it actually is. It is not necessarily as we might prefer it, or understand it, to be. The responsible person tries to eschew wishful thinking and to make the best of her life as it is given to her by reality. And the wise person gladly encounters and examines a plausible new possibility—such as Christianity, authentically understood—and considers carefully whether her existence will be better, before and after death, if lived that way.

And she does well to undertake that investigation sooner, rather than later.

I recognize that this is a Big Ask. "Pondering the meaning of life" is almost comically the very definition of an overwhelming consideration. Contemplating the prospect of changing your life to line it up with significantly different values, allegiances, appetites, and identities? That is a big deal. And, despite all our careful epistemological considerations earlier on, you can't know for sure that you're making the right decision. So it's a big deal *and* fraught with uncertainty.[7]

Worse, it's impossible to fully imagine what it's like to live as a Christian before you've actually done it awhile. We can't imagine in advance what it's really like to parent a new baby, which happens to all sorts of people every day. We can hardly imagine what it would

be like to live seriously in the light of a seriously different and entirely comprehensive Way of Life.[8]

Finally, let's agree that for many of us a conversion to Christianity
would be costly, perhaps even dangerous. Friendships and family
relationships, the esteem of one's peers, job prospects, one's self-
regard—even basic liberty—could be at stake. Conversion has cost
people their lives over the last two millennia, and in no century
more than the last one. So conversion must be considered, let alone
undertaken, with appropriate caution. And Christians ought to be
more sensitive than perhaps we are to the full implications of what
we are so enthusiastically advocating. So, yes, let's recognize that
this is the biggest of big decisions. And you shouldn't make it unless
you've done your due diligence and honestly concluded that you're
ready at least to try this new Way.

But here's hoping you're ready, or will be soon, because I simply
have to ask you: For how many more days do you want to keep
living as you do, rather than as you could?

Notes

Chapter 1

1. Charles Selengut, *Sacred Fury: Understanding Religious Violence* (Walnut Creek, CA: AltaMira, 2003), 6, 44.

2. In this respect, William Cavanaugh's observation is à propos: "Ideologies and institutions labelled secular can be just as absolutist, divisive, and irrational as those labelled religious" (William T. Cavanaugh, *The Myth of Religious Violence: Secular Ideology and the Roots of Modern Conflict* [New York: Oxford University Press, 2009], 6).

3. Among the earliest accounts of such religion is the "Sheilaism" reported by Robert Bellah et al. in their *Habits of the Heart: Individualism and Commitment in American Life* (New York: Harper & Row, 1985).

4. Readers who wonder how "realist" my epistemology is can consult my *Need to Know: Vocation as the Heart of Christian Epistemology* (New York: Oxford University Press, 2014). Perhaps for now it will suffice to locate myself in the cautiously postmodern camp of "critical realists" (although without the slightest debt, so far as I can tell, to Roy Bhaskar, whose work I don't know at all), in the company of those who are deeply impressed by how much our quest for knowledge is affected by our situation, our society, and ourselves. I do not, that is, attempt to argue with all comers on the basis of a strong and wide foundation of common assumptions, since I don't believe such a foundation is available (to any one). Instead, I offer what I can, out of what I think I know, and commend it to my interlocutors for them to examine according to what *they* think *they* know. Among the books that have helped me think this way are Lorraine Code, *Ecological Thinking: The Politics of Epistemic Location* (New York: Oxford University Press, 2006); Michael Polanyi, *Personal Knowledge: Towards a Post-Critical Philosophy* (Chicago: University of Chicago Press, 1958); and Nicholas Wolterstorff, *Reason within the Bounds of Religion*, 2nd ed. (Grand Rapids: Eerdmans, 1984 [1976]).

   At the same time, I can engage lots of different people on enough common ground at least to have a conversation across the lines of our differences. So I eschew the radical postmodernist posturing so helpfully humbled in Alan Sokal and Jean Bricmont, *Fashionable Nonsense: Postmodern Intellectuals' Abuse of Science* (New York: Picador, 1998).

5. Recounting this apothegm is just the most obvious of several places in which I echo William James's famous essay, "The Will to Believe," *The New World* 5 (1896): 327–347.

6. Aristotle, *Posterior Analytics*, 89a.

7. Alvin Plantinga, *Warranted Christian Belief* (New York: Oxford University Press, 2000), 63.

8. Craig M. Gay, *The Way of the (Modern) World: Or, Why It's Tempting to Live as If God Doesn't Exist* (Grand Rapids / Carlisle, UK / Vancouver: Eerdmans / Paternoster / Regent College Publishing, 1998), 305.

9. Philosophers will recognize that this book is, in general, an exercise in inference to the best explanation (abduction), even as deductive and inductive arguments will appear occasionally, and there also will be considerable respect paid toward non-inferential, or "basic," beliefs.

10. Mother Teresa, *Come Be My Light*, ed. Brian Kolodiejchuk (New York: Doubleday Religion, 2007).

Chapter 2

1. Daniel Kahneman, *Thinking, Fast and Slow* (New York: Farrar, Straus & Giroux, 2011), 300–321.

2. An oft-cited set of them is presented in Sarvepalli Radhakrishnan, "History of Indian Thought," introduction to *A Sourcebook in Indian Philosophy*, ed. Sarvepalli Radhakrishnan and Charles A. Moore (Princeton, NJ: Princeton University Press, 1957), xvii–xxxi.

3. According to the Center for the Study of Global Christianity at Gordon-Conwell Theological Seminary in suburban Boston: https://www.gordonconwell.edu/ockenga/ research/ documents/ StatusofGlobalChristianity20191.pdf (accessed 29 March 2019).

4. Justin L. Barrett, *Why Would Anyone Believe in God?* (Lanham, MD: AltaMira, 2004); Justin L. Barrett, *Born Believers: The Science of Children's Religious Belief* (New York: Free Press, 2012); cf. Pascal Boyer, *Religion Explained: The Human Instincts That Fashion God, Spirits, and Ancestors* (London: Vintage, 2002).

5. In this respect, as in so much, New Atheist Sam Harris paints with a spray gun rather than a brush: "While religious people are not

generally mad, their core beliefs absolutely are." I think Harris is wrong about the core beliefs of most of the world's great religions, but I understand why he feels that way about Christianity. See Sam Harris, *The End of Faith: Religion, Terror, and the Future of Reason* (New York: W. W. Norton, 2004), 72.

6. One has in mind the vast tradition of heterodox theologians, familiar contemporary examples of which would be John Spong, Harvey Cox, Rosemary Radford Ruether, Sallie McFague, and the members of the Jesus Seminar.

7. To be sure, Princeton sociologist Robert Wuthnow describes even more mainstream Christians softening the edges, reducing the cultural clashes, and lessening the cognitive scandals of Christianity in *The God Problem: Expressing Faith and Being Reasonable* (Berkeley: University of California Press, 2012). In what follows, we try to avoid any gratuitous shock. But there are nonetheless unavoidable surprises—some would say "absurdities"—in the basics of Christianity that cannot be (cognitively or ethically) bargained away.

8. John H. Walton, *The Lost World of Genesis One: Ancient Cosmology and the Origins Debate* (Downers Grove, IL: InterVarsity, 2009); John C. Lennox, *Seven Days That Divide the World: The Beginning according to Genesis and Science* (Grand Rapids: Zondervan, 2011); Gordon J. Wenham, *Genesis 1–15*, Word Biblical Commentary, vol. 1 (Grand Rapids: Zondervan Academic, 2014); and Hugh C. Ross, *Navigating Genesis: A Scientist's Journey through Genesis 1–11* (Covina, CA: RTB, 2014).

9. I have no scientific expertise, just interest, and so I cannot argue here for the so-called anthropic principle that the universe, our solar system, and our planet are exquisitely, even astonishingly, fine-tuned for the emergence of life and of human life in particular. See John D. Barrow and Frank J. Tipler, *The Anthropic Cosmological Principle* (New York: Oxford University Press, 1986). But other people have noticed what we might call this universe-sized coincidence and argued well for the Christian interpretation of it: Karl W. Giberson, *The Wonder of the Universe: Hints of God in Our Fine-Tuned World* (Downers Grove, IL: InterVarsity, 2012); Alister E. McGrath, *A Fine-Tuned Universe: The Quest for God in Science and Theology*, the 2009 Gifford Lectures (Louisville, KY: Westminster John Knox, 2009); Peter Bussey, *Signposts to God: How Modern Physics and Astronomy Point the Way to Belief* (Downers Grove, IL: InterVarsity, 2016).

10. See Craig M. Gay, "Toward a Theology of Personhood," in *The Way of the (Modern) World: Or, Why It's Tempting to Live as If God Doesn't Exist*

(Grand Rapids / Carlisle, UK / Vancouver: Eerdmans / Paternoster / Regent College Publishing, 1998), 271–313.

11. See Lynn White Jr., "The Historical Roots of Our Ecologic Crisis," *Science* 155 (March 10, 1967): 1203–1207. Cf. Loren Wilkinson, ed., *Earthkeeping in the Nineties: Christian Stewardship of Natural Resources* (Grand Rapids: Eerdmans, 1980); Douglas A. Moo and Jonathan A. Moo, *Creation Care: A Biblical Theology of the Natural World* (Grand Rapids: HarperZondervan, 2018).

12. On the *secularizing* effects of Christianity, see Peter L. Berger, *The Sacred Canopy: Elements of a Sociological Theory of Religion* (Garden City, NY: Anchor, 1969); and Larry W. Hurtado, *Destroyer of the Gods: Early Christian Distinctiveness in the Roman World* (Waco, TX: Baylor University Press, 2016).

13. For similar discussions of shalom and of the world to come, see Nicholas Wolterstorff, *Until Justice and Peace Embrace* (Grand Rapids: Eerdmans, 1983), 69–72; Richard J. Mouw, *When the Kings Come Marching In: Isaiah and the New Jerusalem* (Grand Rapids: Eerdmans, 1983); Paul Marshall, *Heaven Is Not My Home: Living in the Now of God's Creation* (Nashville: Word, 1998); and J. Richard Middleton, *A New Heaven and a New Earth: Reclaiming Biblical Eschatology* (Grand Rapids: Baker Academic, 2014). For a popular account of these ideas, see Randy Alcorn, *Heaven* (Wheaton, IL: Tyndale, 2004).

14. See Hans Boersma, *Seeing God: The Beatific Vision in Christian Tradition* (Grand Rapids: Eerdmans, 2018).

15. Helpful modern studies of sin include the following: Gary A. Anderson, *Sin: A History* (New Haven, CT: Yale University Press, 2009); Alan Jacobs, *Original Sin: A Cultural History* (New York: Harper Collins, 2008); Ted Peters, *Sin: Radical Evil in Soul and Society* (Grand Rapids: Eerdmans, 1994); and Cornelius Plantinga, *Not the Way It's Supposed to Be: A Breviary of Sin* (Grand Rapids: Eerdmans, 1995).

16. Some interpreters have been troubled by the surmise that God killed animals to provide these skins, but presumably God could have taken them from dead animals or even called them out of thin air.

17. To be sure, at a larger level of analysis, *God* is to be held responsible for bringing the whole world, including us and our sinning, into existence. And God does not shirk that responsibility, as the rest of this account makes clear. As to whether God should have sidestepped the whole sorry history of humanity by creating only humans who wouldn't sin—a typical "village atheist" retort to the Christian Story that seems stronger

than it is—see on "the problem of evil" in Chapter 4 in this volume, and my *Can God Be Trusted? Faith and the Challenge of Evil*, rev. ed. (Grand Rapids: InterVarsity, 2008 [1998]).

18. On this history, see Iain Provan, V. Philips Long, and Tremper Longman III, *A Biblical History of Israel*, 2nd ed. (Louisville, KY: Westminster John Knox, 2015). The necessity of understanding the Old Testament in order to make proper sense of the New, and particularly of the Messiah at its focal point, might seem to be obvious, but the point has had to be restated again and again. In our time, the magisterial—nay, the overwhelming—oeuvre of N. T. Wright has done so, extending as he and others have the trajectory of interpretation reaching back at least to E. P. Sanders (originally known for his work on Paul; see esp. E. P. Sanders, *Jesus and Judaism* [London: SCM Press, 1985]).

19. This is the theme of John W. Walton and J. Harvey Walton, *The Lost World of the Torah: Law as Covenant and Wisdom in Ancient Context* (Downers Grove, IL: InterVarsity, 2019).

20. Christianity in modern society has sometimes acted as a brake on the emancipation of women. But Christians were also in the forefront of nineteenth- and twentieth-century campaigns for the rights of women, including the right to vote, but also much more. As law professor Mary Ann Glendon testifies about the longue durée, "When I hear these knee-jerk accusations of sexism in the church, I always want to ask, 'Compared to what other institution?' Wasn't it the Church that gained wide acceptance for the novel idea of marriage as indissoluble—in societies where men had always been permitted by custom to put aside their wives? That fostered the rise of strong, self-governing orders of women religious in the Middle Ages? That pioneered in women's education in countries where most other institutions paid scant attention to girls' intellectual development? No one with the slightest knowledge of history could deny that the advance of Christianity has strengthened the position of women" ("Contrition in the Age of Spin Control," *First Things* [November 1997]: 11). I discuss the historical patterns of Christian treatment of women and why traditional Christian patriarchy should give way to Christian feminism in *Partners in Christ: A Conservative Case for Egalitarianism* (Downers Grove, IL: InterVarsity, 2015).

21. I deal with the issue of God using the cultural materials at hand (in this case, patriarchy) to communicate with people who take such structures for granted, even as God sets out the grounds for undermining of such

structures: see "Inclusive Language," in *Partners in Christ: A Conservative Case for Egalitarianism* (Downers Grove, IL: InterVarsity, 2015), 135–149.

22. Sophisticated analogies for the Trinity, of course, go back at least as far as Augustine. I'm just acknowledging that none of them have commanded anything close to universal agreement as a close, clear, and coherent articulation of what theologians maintain is the *mystery* of the Trinity.

23. The most important study of this subject is Larry W. Hurtado, *Lord Jesus Christ: Devotion to Jesus in Earliest Christianity* (Grand Rapids: Eerdmans, 2005). Some readers will have gathered along the way—perhaps from the arguments of disaffected ex-fundamentalists such as Bart Ehrman—that the idea that Jesus was divine is an exaggeration foisted on Jesus by his overenthusiastic disciples. "Jesus never claimed to be God!" is the usual summary of such arguments. A more moderate version of this debunking comes from even relatively conservative scholars who suggest that Jesus didn't understand himself to be divine.

This question is a complex one, to be sure. But for now, I would mildly suggest that if someone walks like Yhwh and talks like Yhwh, that someone likely is Yhwh. And if his later followers eventually come to that conclusion, why would it be obscure to the person himself?

Jesus not only depends on his Father for the performance of various miracles, but often performs what he calls "signs" by himself, on his own authority: from stilling a storm, thereby signaling mastery over natural forces (Luke 8:22–25); to exorcising a demon, thereby signaling mastery over spiritual forces (Luke 4:31–36); to raising the dead, thereby signaling mastery over life itself (Luke 7:11–16); to forgiving sin, thereby signaling mastery over even the moral realm (Luke 5:20–25). Jesus also makes claims about his relationship with God (John 10:3–39; 14:6–11) and about himself (John 6:27–35, 53–58; 7:28–31; 8:33–39; 11:25–26) that in the Jewish context are unequivocal claims to divinity. The claims are so plain that the stories sometimes end with his auditors furiously attempting to execute him for blasphemy. They understood perfectly well what he was claiming.

Again, I recognize that there is a wide range of disagreement in New Testament studies about all of these matters. But as a theologian possessed of a nodding acquaintance with technical Biblical studies, I'd simply ask, If the early church pretty quickly came to the conclusion, on the basis of what they experienced Jesus to have done and said, that they ought to worship Jesus as Yhwh, why would Jesus—who was doing and saying all those things—somehow not have realized he was Yhwh? The best explanation is the simplest one: He knew.

24. A skeptical reader of this passage in an earlier draft put his dubiety thus: "Actually, it does not seem like a big deal to me. An eternal being spent a few hours on a Friday afternoon suffering a horrible bout of torture, knowing that on Sunday he will be alive and kicking, and that in about 40 days he will be back on his throne being worshipped for all eternity. The whole 'died for our sins' strikes me as one of the greatest ruses in history. It should be, 'Jesus donated a weekend for our sins.'" One might recall, however, the climactic scene in Orwell's *Nineteen Eighty-Four*, during which the protagonist, Winston Smith, experiences the thing he hates and fears the most, a horror that finally breaks him (George Orwell, *Nineteen Eighty-Four* [London: Secker & Warburg, 1949]). Jesus, the only truly innocent person in history, submits to being submerged and smothered in the world's evil, to being crushed to death by the accumulated suffering due the entire human race, enduring an intensity, a *quality*, of suffering that far transcends the *quantity* of time we humans can view him spending on the Cross. (Indeed, since our grasp of time is, at best, elementary, who knows how long Jesus actually suffered?) He suffers and then dies, and he then proceeds even to hell, according to the Apostles' Creed—thus undergoing the experiences we would, and will, experience without his saving us by substituting for us. This experience of Jesus, of which we get only surface glimpses, therefore isn't merely "donating a weekend." This is undergoing a literal world of hurt in an unimaginably telescoped way.

25. Important statements of these themes are John R. W. Stott, *The Cross of Christ* (Downers Grove, IL: InterVarsity, 1986); Fleming Rutledge, *The Crucifixion: Understanding the Death of Jesus Christ* (Grand Rapids: Eerdmans, 2015); and Simon Gathercole, *Defending Substitution: An Essay on Atonement in Paul* (Grand Rapids: Baker Academic, 2015). On hell as the ultimate outcome of those who refuse to link their lives with the only source of life in the cosmos, God, and who refuse to let Jesus pay for their sins and who therefore face the consequences of those sins alone, see Christopher M. Date, Gregory G. Stump, and Joshua W. Anderson, eds., *Rethinking Hell: Readings in Evangelical Conditionalism* (Eugene, OR: Wipf and Stock, 2014); and my contributions to Preston Sprinkle, ed., *Hell: Four Views* (Grand Rapids: HarperZondervan, 2016).

26. For more extensive reflection on what Jesus is teaching on the Sermon on the Mount and particularly in this passage about non-retaliation,

please see my *Making the Best of It: Following Christ in the Real World* (New York: Oxford University Press, 2008), 189–198.

27. This pragmatism helps to explain the degree of social conformity evident in the New Testament in matters such as household slavery and patriarchy. Were the early church to have championed abolition or feminism, inconceivably revolutionary as both causes would have been at that place and time, it would have been crushed without achieving those goals *or* the spread of the gospel. We cannot pause over these matters here, but there is much to read on them: William J. Webb, *Slaves, Women and Homosexuals* (Downers Grove, IL: InterVarsity, 2001); John G. Stackhouse, Jr., *Partners in Christ: A Conservative Case for Egalitarianism* (Downers Grove, IL: InterVarsity, 2015).

28. Indeed, Christian compassion extends to the condemnation of such traditional spectator sports as bear-baiting and cockfighting at least as early as the seventeenth century: Keith Thomas, *Man and the Natural World: Changing Attitudes in England, 1500–1800* (London: Allen Lane, 1983), esp. chap. 4: "Compassion for the Brute Creation." The Christian would recognize with respect the far older doctrine of *ahimsa* (non-injury to other living things) characteristic of traditions in Hinduism, Buddhism, and especially Jainism. To be sure, the end result of *ahimsa*, particularly in Jainism, is a pious suicide by refusing to ingest *anything*. A traditional Christian food ethic, by contrast, that simultaneously validates meat-eating and commands compassionate care for animals may seem both paradoxical but also practical for most people. For broader ethical considerations, see Paul B. Thompson, *From Field to Fork: Food Ethics for Everyone* (New York: Oxford University Press, 2015). And for a Christian ethical defense of vegetarianism, see Charles Camosy, *For Love of Animals: Christian Ethics, Consistent Action* (Cincinnati, OH: Franciscan, 2013).

29. Contemporary atheists often claim that the assertion of universal human rights begins with the atheistic/secularist strands of the Enlightenment and in no way depends on Christian convictions. (The likes of John Rawls, Richard Rorty, and Steven Pinker come readily to mind.) A quick glance at the American Declaration of Independence, among other works, should give one pause about such a claim: "We hold these truths to be self-evident, that all men are created equal, that they are endowed by their Creator with certain unalienable Rights." In fact, the roots of the concept of universal human rights are in the Jewish and Christian Scriptures, and the political implications of these Scriptures for human

rights are first discussed in the (Christian) Middle Ages. See Max L. Stackhouse, *Creeds, Society, and Human Rights: A Study in Three Cultures* (Grand Rapids: Eerdmans, 1984); and Brian Tierney, *The Idea of Natural Rights: Studies on Natural Rights, Natural Law, and Church Law, 1150–1625* (Atlanta: Scholars Press, 1997).

That liberalism cannot long survive cut off from its Christian roots has been argued by many, notably Quaker Elton Trueblood and Jew Will Herberg in the middle of the last century: D. Elton Trueblood, *The Predicament of Modern Man* (New York: Harper & Row, 1944), 59–60; Will Herberg, *Judaism and Modern Man: An Interpretation of Jewish Religion* (New York: Farrar, Straus, & Young, 1951), 91–92. For two more recent expressions, see George Weigel, *The Cube and the Cathedral: Europe, America, and Politics without God* (New York: Basic Books, 2005); and Marcello Pera, *Why We Should Call Ourselves Christians: The Religious Roots of Free Societies*, trans. L. B. Lappin (New York: Encounter, 2011 [2008]). And for a surprising endorsement, here is Jürgen Habermas, in one of his pro-religion moods: "Christianity has functioned for the normative self-understanding of modernity as more than a mere precursor or catalyst. Egalitarian universalism, from which sprang the ideas of freedom and social solidarity, of an autonomous conduct of life and emancipation, of the individual morality of conscience, human rights and democracy, is the direct heir to the Judaic ethic of justice and the Christian ethic of love. This legacy, substantially unchanged, has been the object of continual critical appropriation and reinterpretation. To this day, there is no alternative to it. And in light of the current challenges of a postnational constellation we continue to draw on the substance of this heritage. Everything else is just idle postmodern talk" (*Time of Transitions* [Cambridge: Polity, 2006], 150–151).

Friedrich Nietzsche, of course, agreed also, albeit from a different point of view: *Twilight of the Idols and The Anti-Christ*, trans. R. J. Hollingdale (London: Penguin Books, 1968 [1889/1895]).

30. On the rise of science, human rights, democracy, and other liberating features of modern life arising first in Christian civilization, see the oeuvre by Rodney Stark, a popular-level introduction to which is Rodney Stark, *How the West Won: The Neglected Story of the Triumph of Modernity* (Wilmington, DE: Intercollegiate Studies Institute, 2015).

31. Kenneth Minogue, "Multiculturalism: A Dictatorship of Virtue," introduction to Patrick West, *The Poverty of Multiculturalism* (London: Civitas Institute, 2005), xii.

32. The post-colonial evaluation of the missionary encounter is, however, far from simply bleak. Indeed, the interest of missionaries in protecting local cultures; in the vernacular (as the basic medium of Bible translation and education in Christianity); in the education of all, regardless of class or sex; and in the affirmation of the dignity of each person provided some of the fundamental grounds and tools by which native peoples could negotiate with, and not merely succumb to, the West. See Christopher Hodgkins, *Protestant Colonialism and Conscience in British Literature* (Columbia: University of Missouri Press, 2002); Dana L. Robert, ed., *Converting Colonialism: Visions and Realities in Mission History, 1706–1914* (Grand Rapids: Eerdmans, 2008); Lamin Sanneh, *Whose Religion Is Christianity? The Gospel beyond the West* (Grand Rapids: Eerdmans, 2003); Lamin Sanneh, *Translating the Message: The Missionary Impact on Culture*, 2nd ed. (Maryknoll, NY: Orbis Books, 2009); Olúfémi Táíwò, *How Colonialism Preempted Modernity in Africa* (Bloomington: Indiana University Press, 2010); Andrew F. Walls, *The Missionary Movement in Christian History: Studies in the Transmission of Faith* (Maryknoll, NY / Edinburgh: Orbis / T & T Clark, 2009 [1996]); and Robert D. Woodberry, "The Missionary Roots of Liberal Democracy," *American Political Science Review* 106 (2012): 244–274.

Chapter 3

1. It is thus no coincidence that denial of the historicity of the resurrection and ascension of Jesus always coincides with heterodoxy in other respects as well. I can think of no orthodox Christian thinker of any substance who is even *indifferent* to the historicity of the resurrection and ascension of Jesus.

2. C. A. J. Coady, *Testimony: A Philosophical Study* (Oxford: Clarendon, 1992), 204–205.

3. To be sure, there were very few "professional historians" anywhere in the world before the nineteenth century. There were court chroniclers, of course, who generally amounted to little more than accountants. There were royalty, nobility, generals, and clergy—and, later, gentlemen of leisure—who could afford to take the time to read sources, ponder them, summarize them, and publish them. And there were some who were paid to do it, such as the great Leibniz, who cleverly converted historical commissions into subsidies of his many other pursuits, from mathematics to engineering. The "professor of history," however, is an occupation

widely held only in the nineteenth century, and most of what we have as reliable history in the past was penned by people of quite various trainings and professions. See Ernst Breisach, *Historiography: Ancient, Medieval, and Modern*, 2nd ed. (Chicago: University of Chicago Press, 1994).

4. Alan J. Hauser and Duane F. Watson, eds., *A History of Biblical Interpretation*, vol. 3: *The Enlightenment through the Nineteenth Century* (Grand Rapids: Eerdmans, 2017).

5. Lee Martin McDonald, *The Biblical Canon: Its Origin, Transmission, and Authority*, 3rd ed. (Grand Rapids: Baker Academic, 2007); Craig A. Evans and Emanuel Tov, eds., *Exploring the Origins of the Bible: Canon Formation in Historical, Literary, and Theological Perspective* (Grand Rapids: Baker Academic, 2008).

6. On the historicity and integrity of the New Testament, see (among many volumes) Richard Bauckham, *Jesus and the Eyewitnesses: The Gospels as Eyewitness Testimony* (Grand Rapids: Eerdmans, 2008); Craig L. Blomberg, *The Historical Reliability of the Gospels*, 2nd ed. (Downers Grove, IL: IVP Academic, 2007); Craig L. Blomberg, *The Historical Reliability of the New Testament* (Nashville: B & H Academic, 2016); C. Stephen Evans, *The Historical Christ and the Jesus of Faith: The Incarnational Narrative as History* (Oxford: Clarendon Press, 1996); Elijah Hixson and Peter J. Gurry, eds., *Myths and Mistakes in New Testament Textual Criticism* (Downers Grove, IL: IVP Academic, 2019); and Craig S. Keener, *The Historical Jesus of the Gospels* (Grand Rapids: Eerdmans, 2009).

7. Todd Lake, "My Search for the Historical Jesus," in *Finding God at Harvard: Spiritual Journeys of Thinking Christians*, ed. Kelly Monroe (Grand Rapids: Zondervan, 1996), 44.

8. One skeptical reader of this chapter seemed impressed by the "unknowns" of the situation of Jesus's purported resurrection: "The very often overlooked fact is that there is a lot of evidence that was lost and we simply have no way of knowing whether it was important or not. Luke says 'many' have written about Jesus. Where did all that go? John says that if everything Jesus did was written down, the whole world would not be able to contain it. So even on your own account, a huge bunch of stuff is missing from the record. What enables you to say with such confidence that none of it would've changed the conclusions you've reached about the resurrection?" But this is to put things the wrong way around. The argument here is about what we *do* know. How do we account for the New Testament accounts of Jesus's life, death, and whatever followed? How do we account for the behavior of the disciples after his death? The historian can always wonder what else happened that might change, even radically, her understanding

of her subject. But so what? All she can do is work with what she has. And if she in fact has quite a lot of evidence, and it is both interesting and significant, and it presents a coherent and comprehensive account of what she is trying to understand, then why would she halt her work and say, "But maybe, maybe, there's a completely different interpretation"? What good does that accomplish, especially when she has abundantly good reason to trust the sound historical work she has done—unless, of course, she has come to a conclusion that she finds personally unpalatable? Then my skeptical friend's response makes much more sense.

9. In technical philosophical terms, the early Christians made, and Christians since have made, an inference to the best explanation. There are a lot of data to be explained, and while the agent seems undetectable, the best way to understand what has happened is to infer the activity of that agent. Those trees over there might suddenly have developed sentience and control over their limbs such that they can voluntarily shake them, but most of us, given our experience with such phenomena, would infer instead that the otherwise undetectable wind is blowing through the trees. Likewise, a group such as the early disciples, given their experience and heritage of divine action, readily interpreted these data as indicating God's activity.

10. Coady, *Testimony*, 196. Coady reminds us that this retort from the believer goes back at least as far as William Paley responding to David Hume: "The existence of the testimony is a phenomenon [to be explained]; the truth of the fact [that the miracle actually happened] solves the phenomenon. If we reject the solution, we ought to have some other to rest in; and none . . . can be admitted, which is inconsistent with the principles that regulate human affairs and human conduct at present, or which makes men *then* to have been a different kind of being from what they are now" (*A View of the Evidences of Christianity* [London: n.p., 1953], 36; cited in Coady, *Testimony*, 196–197).

11. Andrew Ter Ern Loke, *The Origin of Divine Christology* (Cambridge: Cambridge University Press, 2017).

12. Harvard biologist Richard Lewontin speaks with refreshing candor: "It is not that the methods and institutions of science somehow compel us to accept a material explanation of the phenomenal world, but, on the contrary, [it is] that we are forced by our a priori adherence to material causes to create an apparatus of investigation and a set of concepts that produce material explanations, no matter how counter-intuitive, no matter how mystifying to the uninitiated. Moreover, that materialism is absolute, for we cannot allow a Divine Foot in the door" ("Billions and Billions

of Demons," *New York Review of Books*, 9 January 1997, https://www.
nybooks.com/articles/1997/01/09/billions-and-billions-of-demons/.
I thank Gerald McDermott for drawing my attention to this article.

13. Mormonism comes to mind, of course, but it sees itself as a version of
Christianity and is obviously indebted to Christianity.

14. G. K. Chesterton, *Orthodoxy* (Garden City, NY: Image/Doubleday, 1959
[1908]), 83.

15. The "cumulative case" approach has a long history, with such notable exponents as Thomas Aquinas, *Summa Contra Gentiles*, trans.
Anton C. Pegis, 5 vols. (Notre Dame, IN: University of Notre Dame
Press, 1955–1957 [written c. 1259–1265]); Joseph Butler, *The Analogy
of Religion* (New York: Frederick Ungar, 1961 [1736]); and Richard
Swinburne, *The Existence of God*, rev. ed. (Oxford: Clarendon, 1991
[1979]).

16. As one who has introduced university students to Buddhism over the
last three decades, I am aware that there is much, much more to the vast
Buddhist tradition than I am suggesting here. But in seeking a simple
comparison I am hewing to the Theravada tradition and to the Four Noble
Truths at the heart of *every* major Buddhist community. I trust that the
knowledgeable reader will concur, as I think the textbooks do as well, with
my brief portrayal of it here.

17. Charles Habib Malik, *A Christian Critique of the University* (Downers
Grove, IL: InterVarsity, 1982), 48.

18. Richard Dawkins, *The God Delusion* (New York: Mariner, 2006), esp.
chaps. 6 and 7.

19. It's not that evolutionary theorists have ignored these questions. Darwin
himself puzzled over beauty. It's that they don't (yet) have a good answer
for these questions. See Alan Jacobs, "Just-So Stories," *Books & Culture*
(January 2013): 19–22; and Ferris Jabr, "How Beauty Is Making Scientists
Rethink Evolution," *New York Times Magazine* (9 January 2019): https://
www.nytimes.com/2019/01/09/magazine/beauty-evolution-animal.html
(accessed 23 February 2019).

20. John Henry Newman, *The Idea of a University* (Notre Dame, IN: University
of Notre Dame Press, 1960 [1852]), 55.

21. Freeman Dyson, "How We Know," *New York Review of Books* 58 (10 March
2011): 10. A century earlier, William James mused thus: "Consciousness
would thus seem in the first instance to be nothing but a sort of superadded
biological perfection,—useless unless it prompted to useful conduct,
and inexplicable apart from that consideration" (*Talks to Teachers on*

Psychology and to Students on Some of Life's Ideals [New York: Henry Holt, 1899], 12).

22. John C. Lennox, *God's Undertaker: Has Science Buried God?* (Oxford: Lion Hudson, 2009 [2007]), 40. Intriguingly, evolutionary psychology can't even deal well (yet?) with sex itself: Elisabeth A. Lloyd, *The Case of the Female Orgasm: Bias in the Science of Evolution* (Cambridge, MA: Harvard University Press, 2006). Even New Atheist philosopher Daniel Dennett admits to succumbing to the charms of music, even especially sacred music, for which he cannot give an adequate account on his own terms: Joshua Rothman, "A Science of the Soul," *The New Yorker* (27 March 2017): 46–55.

23. Rodney Stark, *For the Glory of God: How Monotheism Led to Reformations, Science, Witch-Hunts, and the End of Slavery* (Princeton, NJ: Princeton University Press, 2003), 124–125.

24. William Alston brings this idea into sharper focus: "The cognitive design of human beings represents only one out of a large multitude of possible designs for cognitive subjects, even for embodied cognitive subjects as finite as we, leaving out of account angels and God. It seems clear that there could be corporeal cognitive subjects with forms of sensory receptivity different from ours—sensitivity to different forms of physical energy. There could be subjects with different innate cognitive tendencies, propensities, and hardwired beliefs and concepts. There could be subjects who reason in patterns different from those we employ" (William P. Alston, *A Realist Conception of Truth* [Ithaca, NY: Cornell University Press, 1996], 201).

25. "There is no consistent relation between the degree of scientific advance and a reduced profile of religious influence, belief and practice" (David Martin, "Science and Secularization," in *The Future of Christianity: Reflections on Violence and Democracy, Religion and Secularization* [Farnham, UK: Ashgate, 2011], 121). On Christianity and science, see Arthur James Balfour, *Theism and Humanism* (New York: Hodder and Stoughton, 1915); Alfred North Whitehead, *Science and the Modern World* (New York: Free Press, 1925); Herbert Butterfield, *The Origins of Modern Science, 1300–1800* (Toronto: Clarke, Irwin, 1977 [1951]); R. Hooykaas, *Religion and the Rise of Modern Science* (Grand Rapids: Eerdmans, 1972); Stanley L. Jaki, *Science and Creation: From Eternal Cycles to an Oscillating Universe* (Edinburgh: Scottish Academic Press, 1974); Stark, *For the Glory of God*, chap. 2; Lennox, *God's Undertaker*; and Alvin Plantinga, *Where the Conflict Really Lies: Science, Religion, and Naturalism* (New York: Oxford University Press, 2011).

26. Richard Dawkins, *The God Delusion* (New York: Mariner, 2006). On the "warfare" trope, see Andrew Dickson White, *A History of the Warfare of Science with Theology in Christendom* (New York: D. Appleton, 1896); and Jeff Hardin, Ronald L. Numbers, and Ronald A. Binzley, eds., *The Warfare between Science and Religion: The Idea That Wouldn't Die* (Baltimore, MD: Johns Hopkins University Press, 2018).

27. The ur-text here is Lynn White Jr., "The Historical Roots of Our Ecologic Crisis," *Science* 155 (10 March 1967): 1203–1207.

28. Loren Wilkinson, ed., *Earthkeeping in the Nineties: Christian Stewardship of Natural Resources* (Grand Rapids: Eerdmans, 1980); Leah Kostamo, *Planted: A Story of Creation, Calling, and Community* (Eugene, OR: Wipf & Stock, 2013); Douglas A. Moo and Jonathan A. Moo, *Creation Care: A Biblical Theology of the Natural World* (Grand Rapids: HarperZondervan, 2018).

29. Jacques Ellul, *The Technological Society*, trans. John Wilkinson (New York: Vintage, 1964); Craig M. Gay, *Modern Technology and the Human Future: A Christian Appraisal* (Downers Grove, IL: IVP Academic, 2018). I discuss in *Need to Know* what the Christian ought to do when the deliverances of science and theology do not nicely cohere—as, it must be granted, they sometimes have not and will not.

30. Indeed, sociobiology, evolutionary psychology, and other forms of contemporary scientism fail to offer grounds for why we ought to believe in evolution. For what possible advantage does it afford someone to come up with clever and accurate ideas about the origin of species—*reproductive* advantage, that is? Why would evolution have selected for "ability to think grand theoretical thoughts about huge subjects such as life on earth"? Christianity has a plausible answer for why we can trust our brains to develop reliable theories, an answer rooted in human beings being called by their Maker to care for the world, which involves, among other things, the deepest and clearest understanding of the world obtainable. But evolution on its own terms? One doesn't have to be uncharitable to doubt that a great facility in theoretical thought is not generally seen to accrue to a person's reproductive advantage. See C. S. Lewis, "De Futilitate," in *Christian Reflections*, ed. Walter Hooper (Grand Rapids: Eerdmans, 1967 [1943]), 57–71; and Plantinga, *Where the Conflict Really Lies*. Intriguingly, even Dawkins confesses to an evolutionarily prompted skepticism in the conclusion of *The God Delusion*.

31. David Hume, "Of Miracles," in *An Enquiry concerning Human Understanding*, section X (1748).

32. Among many other retorts, see J. Houston, *Reported Miracles: A Critique of Hume* (Cambridge: Cambridge University Press, 1994); and Robert A. Larmer, *The Legitimacy of Miracle* (Lanham, MD: Lexington, 2014).

33. This line of response, that context matters greatly in the assessment of testimony to miracles, goes back at least as far as Antoine Arnauld, who inspired Blaise Pascal. For a treatment sympathetic to the view I express here that deals economically with a wide range of thinkers—including John Locke, David Hume, Pierre Laplace, William Paley, John Stuart Mill, and even G. K. Chesterton—see C. A. J. Coady, "Astonishing Reports," in *Testimony: A Philosophical Study* (Oxford: Clarendon, 1992), 179–198. Perhaps the most aggressive version of this argument, based particularly on probability theory, is Richard Swinburne, *The Resurrection of God Incarnate* (Oxford: Clarendon, 2003). (One doesn't have to subscribe to the particulars of Swinburne's Bayesian mathematics to feel the force of his overall argument.) See also Craig S. Keener, *Miracles: The Credibility of the New Testament Accounts*, 2 vols. (Grand Rapids: Baker Academic, 2011).

34. James Davison Hunter and Paul Nedelisky, *Science and the Good: The Tragic Quest for the Foundations of Morality* (New Haven, CT: Yale University Press, 2018).

35. See the classic essays by literary scholar C. S. Lewis, "De Futilitate," in C. S. Lewis, *Christian Reflections*, ed. Walter Hooper (Grand Rapids: Eerdmans, 1967 [1943]), 57–71; philosopher G. E. M. Anscombe, "Modern Moral Philosophy," *Philosophy* 33 (January 1958): 1–19; and political scientist Glenn Tinder, "Can We Be Good without God? On the Political Meaning of Christianity," *The Atlantic* (December 1989), https://www.theatlantic.com/ magazine/archive/ 1989/12/can-we-be-good-without-god/306721/. Tinder expanded this discussion in *The Political Meaning of Christianity: An Interpretation* (Baton Rouge: Louisiana State University Press, 1989). For a more recent statement of how atheists have to "smuggle in" Christian values to make their ethics work, see law professor Steven D. Smith, *The Disenchantment of Secular Discourse* (Cambridge, MA: Harvard University Press, 2010). And even the eloquent statement by Ronald Dworkin, *Religion without God* (Cambridge, MA: Harvard University Press, 2013), takes us no further than an atheist sensing and affirming, as others have, a transcendent metaphysical, moral, and aesthetic order—but sensing and affirming aren't the same things as reliably and coherently articulating and explaining. That's what theism, and Christianity in particular, can do that atheism cannot. On different

types of atheism, see the recent taxonomy in John Gray, *Seven Types of Atheism* (New York: Farrar, Straus and Giroux, 2018).

36. Martin Luther, *The Freedom of a Christian* (1520).

37. For this genealogy of "agapism," see part 1 of Nicholas Wolterstorff, *Justice in Love* (Grand Rapids: Eerdmans, 2011).

38. I discuss this concept in my two books on ethics: *Making the Best of It: Following Christ in the Real World* (New York: Oxford University Press, 2008); and, in a revised and more popular form, *Why You're Here: Ethics for the Real World* (New York: Oxford University Press, 2018).

39. In his study of charity in the Biblical tradition, Gary Anderson cites Paul Veyne in this respect: "What made the charitable works of the church distinctive was their religious grounding and singular focus on the abject poor. In contrast, Greco-Roman benefactors had little interest in helping the lower social classes and did not think of their donations as having a religious function. Homes for the elderly, orphanages, and hospitals, Veyne observes, are institutions that appeared suddenly in the late Roman era and always in the wake of the expansion of the Christian church. New words, in fact, had to be invented in both Latin and Greek to identify these charitable organizations, a sure sign that they had no precedent; they were the fruits of this new religion" (Gary A. Anderson, *Charity: The Place of the Poor in the Biblical Tradition* [New Haven, CT: Yale University Press, 2013], 16; citing Paul Veyne, *Bread and Circuses* [London: Penguin, 1976], 33).

40. On these themes, see the following: Miroslav Volf, *Exclusion & Embrace: A Theological Exploration of Identity, Otherness, and Reconciliation* (Nashville: Abingdon, 1996); Miroslav Volf, *Free of Charge: Giving and Forgiving in a Culture Stripped of Grace* (Grand Rapids: Zondervan, 2005); and Jonathan Hill, *What Has Christianity Ever Done for Us? How It Shaped the Modern World* (Downers Grove, IL: InterVarsity, 2005).

41. Lamin Sanneh, *Translating the Message: The Missionary Impact on Culture*, 2nd ed. (Maryknoll, NY: Orbis, 2009 [1989]), 11.

42. Some still entertain the notion that religion is peculiarly inclined to promote violence—a claim that was far more plausible when made by the likes of Baron d'Holbach and other atheistic *philosophes* in the eighteenth century than in our own time, after the bloodiest century in history whose horrors were largely prosecuted in the name of secular ideologies. Those seeking true enlightenment on such matters should consult the following: David Martin, *Does Christianity Cause War?* (Oxford: Clarendon, 1997); David Martin, *Religion and Power: No Logos without Mythos*

(Farnham, UK: Ashgate, 2014), esp. part 1: "Religion, War and Violence"; Alan Jacobs and Kenneth Chase, eds., *Must Christianity Be Violent? Reflections on History, Practice, and Theology* (Grand Rapids: Brazos, 2003); and William T. Cavanaugh, *The Myth of Religious Violence: Secular Ideology and the Roots of Modern Conflict* (New York: Oxford University Press, 2009).

43. Sociologist David Martin remarks wryly that "if the peoples of the Ottoman empire appealed to the Koran or to the principles of the Ottomans to relieve their subordination, I am unaware of it" (David Martin, *On Secularization: Towards a Revised General Theory* [Burlington, VT: Ashgate, 2005], 166). I know Martin would agree that the principle holds in both directions for other religions and cultures: Bharatiya Janata Party Hindus campaign consistently for Hindutva in India, while oppressive Buddhist regimes in Southeast Asia stand condemned by the ethics of the religion they claim to uphold.

44. Philosopher Linda Zagzebski comments, "The experience of knowing holy people is still the most important evidence to me for the truth of Christianity" ("Vocatio Philosophiae," in *Philosophers Who Believe*, ed. Kelly James [Downers Grove, IL: InterVarsity, 1993], 239.) Mother (now Saint) Teresa of Calcutta is perhaps the most famous holy Christian of our time, and the edition of her private writings, which reveals her difficulties in faith while maintaining a heroic ministry, only adds to the luster of her testimony. As one of her confessors says, "Whenever I met Mother, all self-consciousness left me. I felt right away at ease: she radiated peace and joy, even when she shared with me the darkness in her spiritual life. I was often amazed that someone who lived so much face to face with suffering people and went through a dark night herself still could smile and make you feel happy. . . . I believe that I can say that I felt in God's presence, in the presence of truth and love" (Father Michael van der Peet; quoted in Mother Teresa, *Come Be My Light*, ed. Brian Kolodiejchuk [New York: Doubleday Religion, 2007], 269).

45. For two recent studies, see Simone Croezen et al., "Social Participation and Depression in Old Age: A Fixed-Effects Analysis in 10 European Countries," *American Journal of Epidemiology* 182 (15 July 2015): 168–176; and Eric S. Kim and Tyler J. VanderWeele, "Mediators of the Association between Religious Service Attendance and Mortality," *American Journal of Epidemiology* 188 (January 2019): 96–101. These large generalizations hold true even for teenagers. See Christian Smith and Melinda Lundquist

Denton, *Soul Searching: The Religious and Spiritual Lives of American Teenagers* (New York: Oxford University Press, 2005).

46. Kurt Bowen, *Christians in a Secular World: The Canadian Experience* (Montreal: McGill-Queen's University Press, 2004), 181, 288; cf. Peter V. Marsden, ed., *Social Trends in American Life: Findings from the General Social Survey since 1972* (Princeton, NJ: Princeton University Press, 2012); Pew Research Center, "Religion's Relationship to Happiness, Civic Engagement and Health around the World" (31 January 2019), https://www.pewforum.org/2019/01/31/religions-relationship-to-happiness-civic-engagement-and-health-around-the-world/.

47. Nancy Nason-Clark et al., *Religion and Intimate Partner Violence: Understanding the Challenges and Proposing Solutions* (New York: Oxford University Press, 2017).

48. I don't mean to indulge in the "no true Scotsman" fallacy here. What I offer is, I trust, simply common sense. If you want to encounter jazz, start with Louis Armstrong or Wynton Marsalis. If you want to investigate automobiles, consider Porsche or Ferrari.

49. John Howard Yoder, *The Priestly Kingdom: Social Ethics as Gospel* (Notre Dame, IN: University of Notre Dame Press, 1985), 94.

50. See Peter and Linda Murray, *The Oxford Companion to Christian Art and Architecture* (Oxford: Oxford University Press, 1996).

51. I say more about intuition, imagination, and art in epistemology here: *Need to Know: Vocation as the Heart of Christian Epistemology* (New York: Oxford University Press, 2014), 109–111, 127–133. See also Iain McGilchrist, *The Master and His Emissary: The Divided Brain and the Making of the Western World* (New Haven, CT: Yale University Press, 2009).

52. With these cautions in mind about too readily linking beauty and truth, one can appreciate the rich meditations of Thomas Dubay, *The Evidential Power of Beauty: Science and Theology Meet* (San Francisco: Ignatius Press, 1999); and Elaine Scarry, *On Beauty and Being Just* (Princeton, NJ: Princeton University Press, 1999).

53. Mihaly Csikszentmihalyi, *Creativity: Flow and the Psychology of Discovery and Invention* (New York: Harper, 1996).

54. Steven D. Smith, *The Disenchantment of Secular Discourse* (Cambridge, MA: Harvard University Press, 2010), 205. Critic George Steiner, himself no orthodox believer, testifies similarly to the dependence of most of the great art of our culture on a sense of "a divine presence" (*Real Presences*

[Chicago: University of Chicago Press, 1989]; and *Errata: An Examined Life* [New Haven, CT: Yale University Press, 1997], esp. 181–190).

55. See Abigail Woolley, "Art's Claim on Resources: Sabbath Ethics as a Framework for Value," *The Journal of Scriptural Reasoning* 16 (June 2017): https://jsr.shanti.virginia.edu/back-issues/volume-16-no-1-june-2017-recent-reflections-on-scriptural-reasoning/arts-claim-on-resources-sabbath-ethics-as-a-framework-for-value/. An earlier statement is H. R. Rookmaaker, *Art Needs No Justification* (Downers Grove, IL: InterVarsity, 1978).

56. Nicholas Wolterstorff, *Art in Action* (Grand Rapids: Eerdmans, 1980).

57. I discuss the universal human calling to make shalom in *Making the Best of It: Following Christ in the Real World* (New York: Oxford University Press, 2008); and in *Why You're Here: Ethics for the Real World* (New York: Oxford University Press, 2018).

58. For two very different discussions of the importance of feelings and needs in considering religion, see Clifford Williams, *Existential Reasons for Belief in God: A Defense of Desires and Emotions for Faith* (Downers Grove, IL: InterVarsity, 2011); and Francis Spufford, *Unapologetic: Why, Despite Everything, Christianity Can Still Make Surprising Emotional Sense* (San Francisco: HarperOne, 2013).

59. Such a validation stands in sharp contrast to the reductionism offered us by sociobiology and other forms of materialism, scientism, or naturalism. As David Martin mournfully asks, "Are the last words 'Nothing but'—nothing but genes or programming or social process?" (*Christian Language in the Secular City* [Aldershot, UK: Ashgate, 2002], 74).

60. This theme—of the interconnection of the rational, the moral, the intuitive, the experiential, the mystical, the extraordinary, and the daily—courses throughout the work of the last century's pre-eminent defender and commender of the Christian faith, C. S. Lewis. That theme thus recurs throughout George M. Marsden, *C. S. Lewis's Mere Christianity: A Biography* (Princeton, NJ: Princeton University Press, 2016).

61. A classic manual to such experience is Nicolas Herman (Brother Lawrence of the Resurrection), *Writings and Conversations on the Practice of the Presence of God*, trans. Salvatore Sciurba, OCD (Washington, DC: Institute of Carmelite Studies, 1994).

62. The classic Christian inquiry into such matters is Rudolf Otto, *The Idea of the Holy*, trans. John W. Harvey, 2nd ed. (New York: Oxford University Press, 1950 [1923]).

63. Phillip H. Wiebe, *Visions of Jesus: Direct Encounters from the New Testament to Today* (Oxford: Oxford University Press, 1997).

64. The most important philosophical defense of such beliefs is William P. Alston, *Perceiving God: The Epistemology of Religious Experience* (Ithaca, NY: Cornell University Press, 1991). See also Keith E. Yandell, "Monotheism and Religious Experience," in *Philosophy of Religion: A Contemporary Introduction* (New York: Routledge, 1999), 215–235; Richard Swinburne, "The Argument from Religious Experience," in *The Existence of God*, 2nd ed. (Oxford: Oxford University Press, 2004), 293–327; Michael Sudduth, "The Contribution of Religious Experience to Dogmatic Theology," in *Analytic Theology: New Essays in the Philosophy of Theology*, ed. Oliver D. Crisp and Michael E. Rea (New York: Oxford University Press, 2009), 214–232; and Philip H. Wiebe, *Intuitive Knowing as Spiritual Experience* (London: Palgrave Macmillan, 2015).

65. Kelly James Clark, ed., *Philosophers Who Believe* (Downers Grove, IL: InterVarsity, 1993); Thomas V. Morris, ed., *God and the Philosophers* (New York: Oxford University Press, 1994). See also the many similar testimonies in Kelly Monroe, ed., *Finding God at Harvard: Spiritual Journeys of Thinking Christians* (Grand Rapids: Zondervan, 1996).

66. Peter van Inwagen, "Quam Dilecta," in *God and the Philosophers*, ed. Thomas V. Morris (New York: Oxford University Press, 1994), 33.

67. Van Inwagen, "Quam Dilecta," 36.

68. Van Inwagen, "Quam Dilecta," 36.

69. William P. Alston, "A Philosopher's Way Back to the Faith," in *God and the Philosophers*, ed. Thomas V. Morris (New York: Oxford University Press, 1994), 20.

70. Alston, "A Philosopher's Way," 21.

71. Alston, "A Philosopher's Way," 22.

72. Alston, "A Philosopher's Way," 22.

73. Alston, "A Philosopher's Way," 27.

74. Contemporary testimonies of this sort range from C. S. Lewis's modern classic, *Surprised by Joy: The Shape of My Early Life* (New York: Harcourt Brace Jovanovich, 1955), to Christian Wiman's moving *My Bright Abyss: Meditation of a Modern Believer* (New York: Farrar, Straus and Giroux, 2013). Cf. the testimony of Antony Flew, who converted from atheism to deism, if not (so far as the record shows) to Christianity: Antony Flew, *There Is a God: How the World's Most Notorious Atheist Changed His Mind* (San Francisco: HarperOne, 2007). Regarding Flew and Christianity, however, one notes with curiosity the last appendix in the book: a dialogue

between Flew and the acclaimed New Testament scholar N. T. Wright, the scholar whom Flew praises as presenting "by far the best case for accepting Christian belief that I have ever seen" (3).

75. Again, I certainly do not want to over-claim. Former Regius Professor of Divinity at Cambridge University David Ford presumably had considerable experience in assessing and asserting the rational grounds for Christian belief, and yet he concludes, "Highly intelligent people still argue endlessly about the best way to conceive reality. After decades spent studying, teaching, taking part in debates and conversations in universities in Europe, North America, and elsewhere, I have come to one obvious conclusion: people who are as intelligent as each other, as well educated as each other, and as historically, scientifically, and philosophically literate as each other can still come to fundamentally different convictions and worldviews. In other words, these ultimate questions are never likely to be decided to everyone's satisfaction by history, science, philosophy, or any other discipline or combination of disciplines. There are all sorts of ways of trying to win the arguments, new evidence is constantly being introduced, and intellectual fashions change (and are far more influential than intellectuals tend to think), but the idea that 'all right-thinking people' are ever going to agree on such matters is unimaginable" (David F. Ford, *The Drama of Living: Becoming Wise in the Spirit* [Grand Rapids: Brazos Press, 2014], 128).

Chapter 4

1. See the Parliament of the World's Religions, *Towards a Global Ethic: An Initial Declaration of the Parliament of the World's Religions* (1993; revised 2018), https://parliamentofreligions.org /sites/default/files/Global%20 Ethic%20booklet-update-web_0.pdf. I have offered some thoughts on these questions relevant to my home country of Canada here: "Of Course Canada Is a 'Secular' State—Just Not Secularist and Only Partly Secularized," *Journal of Parliamentary and Political Law / Revue de droit parlementaire et politique* 7 (July 2013): 189–199.

2. William P. Alston, *Perceiving God: The Epistemology of Religious Experience* (Ithaca, NY: Cornell University Press, 1991), 267.

3. The life's work of philosopher John Hick stands as a cautionary tale. Hick was unable to convince even a majority of his fellow scholars of religion that he had identified the common element(s) of all (major) religions, let alone make any inroads among serious, informed believers in the rank and

file. See John Hick, *An Interpretation of Religion: Human Responses to the Transcendent* (New Haven, CT: Yale University Press, 1989); and *A Christian Theology of Religions: The Rainbow of Faiths* (Louisville, KY: Westminster John Knox Press, 1995). A similar commendation of a "religion-in-general" made a generation or so earlier is John Dewey, *A Common Faith* (New Haven, CT: Yale University Press, 1934). And for more recent attempts, see the one inspired by Jacques Derrida's notion of a perpetually indeterminate faith by John Caputo, *On Religion* (New York: Routledge, 2001); plus the panentheistic offering of Mark Johnston, *Saving God: Religion after Idolatry* (Princeton, NJ: Princeton University Press, 2011 [2009]). Among many critiques of such views, see Keith E. Yandell, *Philosophy of Religion: A Contemporary Introduction* (New York: Routledge, 1999), esp. chap. 6.

4. This is the orthodox Christian answer to G. E. Lessing's famous fear of the "ugly broad ditch" (*der garstige breite Graben*) between history and religion (Gotthold Ephraim Lessing, "On the Proof of the Spirit and of Power," in *Philosophical and Theological Writings*, trans. and ed. H. B. Nisbet [Cambridge: Cambridge University Press, 2005], 87). Lessing was confident, as so many have been, that ultimate religious truth must be everywhere equally distributed and intelligible to any rational person. The various religions of the world thus are merely local apprehensions of these timeless verities. Lessing's famous play *Nathan the Wise* (1779) makes these points vividly.

But Christianity doesn't share with Lessing the underlying assumption that what we human beings need most from religion is a clear conception of ultimate truth, to which we will then happily conform our lives. Christianity instead affirms that we are sinners who have placed ourselves into a hopeless state from which we need God to stage a mighty act of rescue. That act, as a historical occurrence, must ipso facto occur. It must happen in a particular time and place. The Gospel asserts that that act has occurred and identifies the location—in history.

5. For reflections on the political implications of the Ascension of Christ, see Oliver O'Donovan, *The Desire of the Nations: Rediscovering the Roots of Political Thought* (Cambridge: Cambridge University Press, 1996), 141–162. On the history of Christian understanding of the Ascension, see Douglas Farrow, *Ascension & Ecclesia: On the Significance of the Doctrine of Ascension* (Edinburgh: T. & T. Clark, 1999); and Douglas Farrow, *Ascension Theology* (Edinburgh: T. & T. Clark, 2011).

6. Søren Kierkegaard, *Practice in Christianity*, trans. Howard V. Hong and Edna H. Hong (Princeton, NJ: Princeton University Press, 1991 [1850]), 98.

7. Penn Jillette, "A Gift of a Bible," https://www.youtube.com/watch?v=6md638smQd8 (accessed 23 March 2018). For a scholarly discussion of this logic, see Paul J. Griffiths, *An Apology for Apologetics: A Study in the Logic of Interreligious Dialogue* (Maryknoll, NY: Orbis, 1991). West African scholar Lamin Sanneh tells Western Christians to get over their enervating feelings of guilt and share the gospel in *Whose Religion Is Christianity? The Gospel beyond the West* (Grand Rapids: Eerdmans, 2003).

8. Clark H. Pinnock, *A Wideness in God's Mercy: The Finality of Jesus Christ in a World of Religions* (Grand Rapids: Zondervan, 1992); John G. Stackhouse, Jr., "An Agenda for an Evangelical Theology of Religions," in *No Other Gods before Me? Evangelicals Confront the World's Religions*, ed. John G. Stackhouse, Jr. (Grand Rapids: Baker Academic, 2001), 189–201. Alert readers will note that I have not yet addressed the last element in that third objection, namely, "*eternal* torture in hell." Historically, Christians have held two main views: the majority view is that those not availing themselves of Jesus's substitution for them will suffer forever, while the minority view is that such people will indeed pay for their sins in suffering, but since a human being can commit only a finite amount of sin, thus incurring only a finite amount of sinning, it seems illogical and unjust to believe in *never-ending* suffering. For this debate, see Preston Sprinkle, ed., *Four Views on Hell* (Grand Rapids: HarperZondervan, 2016). Spoiler: I defend in that book the minority view.

9. See my *Can God Be Trusted?*; C. S. Lewis, *The Problem of Pain* (New York: Collier, 1962); and Alvin Plantinga, *God, Freedom, and Evil* (Grand Rapids: Eerdmans, 1974).

10. Christopher Hitchens was capable of considered and vivacious literary criticism, but he gives full vent to adolescent pique at every turn in his bestselling rant that, among its many embarrassing stupidities, is full of locutions of the "A creative deity, of course, would have—" variety (*God Is Not Great: How Religion Poisons Everything* [Toronto: McClelland & Stewart, 2007], 84). For a more temperate version, see Stephen Jay Gould, *The Panda's Thumb: More Reflections in Natural History* (New York: W. W. Norton, 1980). This is a rhetorical tradition going back in modern times at least as far as Hume's *Dialogues concerning Natural Religion* (1779).

Chapter 5

1. William James, "The Will to Believe," *New World* 5 (June 1896): 327–347.

2. The classic text of this sort is C. S. Lewis, *Mere Christianity* (New York: HarperSanFrancisco, 1980 [1952]). More recent commendations are

Timothy Keller, *The Reason for God: Belief in an Age of Skepticism* (New York: Penguin, 2008); Francis Spufford, *Unapologetic: Why, Despite Everything, Christianity Can Still Make Surprising Emotional Sense* (San Francisco: HarperOne, 2013); and N. T. Wright, *Simply Christian: Why Christianity Makes Sense* (San Francisco: HarperSanFrancisco, 2006).

3. The text I recommend is Theodore Ludwig, *The Sacred Paths: Understanding the Religions of the World*, 4th ed. (Upper Saddle River, NJ: Prentice Hall, 2006 [1989]).

4. "All legitimations of death must carry out the same essential task—they must enable the individual to go on living in society after the death of significant others and to anticipate his own death with, at the very least, terror sufficiently mitigated so as not to paralyze the continued performance of the routines of everyday life." Peter L. Berger and Thomas Luckmann, *The Social Construction of Reality: A Treatise in the Sociology of Knowledge* (Garden City, NJ: Doubleday, 1966), both quotations from 101.

   Glenn Tinder is eloquent on this theme: "Dying has an essential role in what might be called God's pedagogy of hope. Death divests us of every finite source of security, that is, of every idol. It leaves us altogether without refuge or resources. In doing this it defeats pride definitively, for it strips us of the very powers by which resources are used. It is the last humiliation. Death thus creates a situation in which we must either trust in God or give up hope. Glenn Tinder, *The Fabric of Hope: An Essay* (Atlanta: Scholars Press, 1999), 143.

   Friedrich Nietzsche, of course, gives up hope. He mocks those who fear "that monstrous adversary, time" and their "longing for immortality: riches, power, intelligence, quickness of mind, eloquence, a healthy appearance, a famous name—all these are merely means by which the insatiable personal life force yearns for new life, thirsts for an ultimately illusory immortality." (Friedrich Nietzsche, *Anti-Education*, ed. Paul Reitter and Chad Wellmon [New York: New York Review of Books, 2016 (1872)], 54–55).

5. Rebecca Mead, "Prophet of Dystopia," *The New Yorker* (17 April 2017): 47.

6. Glenn Tinder observes, "The worst situations are not necessarily those that cause the most intense immediate suffering but those that seem to take away the future" (*The Political Meaning of Christianity: An Interpretation* [Baton Rouge: Louisiana State University Press, 1989], 232).

7. William Alston sympathizes: "Many factors can prevent someone from appreciating the strength of an argument. It may be difficult to hold it before the mind all at once and grasp the way in which the parts fit together. There may be strong contrary prejudices from group opinion or early

training. Furthermore, philosophical argumentation, especially in metaphysics, is the opposite of cut-and-dried. It takes mature, sensitive judgment to appreciate its force. And finally, there may be truths that some people are simply not capable of seeing" (William P. Alston, *A Realist Conception of Truth* [Ithaca, NY: Cornell University Press, 1996), 169. We recall encountering the fact, to be sure, that Alston himself, a notable analytic philosopher, came to Christian faith *not* primarily because of such argument, but due to the combined impetus of a number of experiences, including mystical ones, in his life. So deciding about Christianity has all the challenge of considering the adoption of a very different philosophical system—and then some.

8. Joshua Rothman, "Choose Wisely," *The New Yorker* (21 January 2019): 26–31.